Food, Farm and Garden Funding:

300+ Grants, Scholarships and More

in the U.S. and Canada

Authored By:
PAMELA BURKE

ISBN-13:978-1511448062

ISBN-10:1511448067

DEDICATION

This book is dedicated to my parents and the other hard working farm families with whom I grew up and to the new entrepreneurial farmers that are testing new sustainable methods while changing the face of food production.

CONTENTS

ACKNOWLEDGEMENTS
Authored By:
PAMELA BURKE, LLC
GRANTS CONSULTANT ~ FUND DEVELOPMENT + GRANT
RESEARCH/WRITING
Over 35 years experience
_Improving the quality of life for communities by building organizational
capacity_
Phone (989) 330-1678; Email info@grant-write.com;
website www.grant-write.com

Research editing by Clara Bauman - dadsit90@gmail.com
Graphic Design by Audrea DeLong - asd.design35@gmail.com
Farm Vegetables Cover Photo - © IStock.com/gpointestudio

Printed by CreateSpace, an Amazon.com Company;
Available from Amazon.com, CreateSpace.com, and,
through www.grant-write.com.

INTRODUCTION:

All across North America there is a growing interest in foods produced locally and sustainably. People want access to fresh foods with good quality that are affordable. Working together, neighbors and classroom children take delight in establishing community and school gardens. Farm markets, farm stands, cooperatives, food events and buying clubs like community supported agriculture offer a unique food buying experience. Shoppers enjoy meeting the folks that produce their food. Buyers like to know where and how food was produced. Collaborative efforts can improve marketing, storage and delivery systems for producers. With education and guidance, new entrepreneurial farmers and artisans can creatively add value to home grown products sold in area restaurants, stores and markets. Offering healthier menu options is now the norm. The missing key ingredient is often funding.

USING THE FUNDING DIRECTORY & WRITING A GRANT

The purpose of this directory is to **save you hundreds of hours** searching for funders who have shown an interest in your cause. Funders can be foundations, trusts, funds within community foundations, corporate giving programs, associations, nonprofit organizations and governmental agencies. Funding may be available in the form of a loan, a grant, a donation, a contract for services, a cooperative agreement, or a scholarship.

Consider the odds. If a funder publishes that there will only be four awards made during the year (as opposed to 40), unless your project is exactly what the funder wishes to support, the odds of getting awarded diminishes. Because there are many more nonprofits seeking funding than there are funders, grant funding should be only one of your sources of revenue. Most funders like to invest in established organizations; fewer funders make awards to new nonprofits or wish to pay for operating day to day costs.

Increase your odds. Study your funder before applying. Follow the funder's directions. Make sure the contact person's information is clearly included. Make sure your math is correct. Do your homework to make sure the funder's passion is your passion – How much do they typically award? How many awards were made last year? And where?

If you have the opportunity to speak or correspond with the funder, please do so. Ask the funder to describe the best project ever funded – the one that makes them most proud. Run your idea past them before you put in a great deal of effort. Confirm the deadline and how the funder wants it to be submitted (Send a letter of inquiry first briefly describing the project and then wait for an invitation? Send by email? Online form? Typed? Certain font? Single spaced or doubled? Limit on the number of pages allowed? By U.S. mail or another mail delivery service (and are there different addresses such as a P.O. Box or a street address.) Delivered by a certain date and time? Signature in ink or will an electronic signature work? Multiple copies of proposal but just one set of attachments?) Also ask, when is the start date and when is the end date. All funders have different grant periods which often do not match your organization's fiscal year.

First things first...are you eligible? Each funder will state who is eligible for their grants. Most grants are awarded to nonprofit organizations or local governments for charitable or educational purposes. Sometimes a local government or nonprofit is the applicant on behalf of a group; the nonprofit may write a for-profit business or provider (farm, animal rescue, etc.) or group of providers into the grant project as contractual providers. Scholarships are usually awarded to individuals. Loans and contracts may be available to individuals, for-profit businesses/providers and nonprofit organizations.

Is your organization ready to apply for a grant? Grant readiness is key. Funders may ask for certain documents to be included with your proposal so that they can determine your organization's readiness and management competence. Do you or your fiduciary have paper and/or digitized copies of your organization's legal, governance and financial documents at the ready? These may include the organizational EIN#, 501c3 letter, Financial Statement/Audit, Annual Budget, and Board Roster? Some funders may also ask to see some of these: By-Laws, Articles of Incorporation, DUNS #, Proof of Liability Insurance, Fund Development/ Donor recognition plan, Staff bios/Resumes', Organizational Chart, Mission/values statement, and/or, an Annual Report. I suggest scanning these docs and keeping them in a folder in the computer for easy retrieval. You will also look use these docs for certain information required on online application forms, for filling out paper grant forms, or, as Attachments. Does your organization have the skills and resources to manage a grant? Does your organization have the ability to track restricted funds in your bookkeeping system?

When writing a grant, keep in mind that you are competing against many other applicants. Don't assume that the grant reviewer understands your community or your system. Make sure there are no misspelled words. Make sure that all acronyms are defined. And that information follows logically.

It is important to use words that "paint a picture" for the reader when describing the community to be served, the setting and the problem to be solved. You will then explain your proposed solution to the problem and what resources and expertise your organization will use to address it.

Research is the first step in finding funding. Locating funders that may be interested in your cause, your activity and location can be extremely time consuming. After circling the best prospective funders, do even more research by reading the funder's website – especially their "About Us" section, Giving Guidelines, and past awardees. Their annual reports will also provide information about the approaches they most often support.

Awards are made to satisfy the donor's desire. Keep in mind that you are not only seeking a grant to enhance your program to better serve your community, but to **meet the funder's intended purpose**. Note those funders that provide funding *where* you wish to operate your program, that are interested in *what* you wish to accomplish and *when*.

Look for those whose application process meets your timeline. One to six months can pass between the day you submit your application and the date of the funder's response. And your official start date can be even later. So think ahead and try to seek funding for your next fiscal year.

Some funders reserve most or all of their awards to certain *STATES* or *PROVINCES*. If funders in this directory restrict their awards geographically these are shown in CAPS.

Also note that some funders may only accept grants during certain windows of time, may have deadlines or giving cycles. Funders may change their deadlines and application processes so check their website and follow the instructions as published. Once you find some funders in the directory with whom you have a connection you can begin building a quarterly calendar. If possible begin working on the grant in the quarter before the expected due date.

Funders make grants and scholarship awards to promote the cause near and dear to them. Look for funders with whom you sense a connection. As you review the entries in this directory, look for those that best match your ideals, proposed activity, your approach, and, geographic area of interest.

Grants tend to follow the same general order. You may wish to begin with a powerful attention getting statement. Example: "The food safety of meat, milk, cheese and eggs is threatened by the shortage of veterinarians treating farm animals in the state. Some estimates say that only one out of forty practicing vets currently treat farm animals."

Grant proposals generally contain the following:

The issue, problem, or need,

Who is impacted, how many/where, and who will benefit,

Who you are (about your organization, mission/values, governance, service area/community, experience),

What (proposed solution, goal/objectives, desired outcomes),

How (activities, who will do what to whom and how often, the process),

When (project start & end date, timeline),

How much (costs, resources, the $ request), how you will measure success (process, outputs, outcomes),

Impact/Sustainability,

Staffing/Chances of Succeeding (Credentials? Memberships? Staff expertise and training? Who will supervise? Systems in place? Partnerships?) .

Some examples of problems that your proposal may address:

FOOD/FARMS/GARDENS PROBLEMS	
Distance to access fresh foods	Unhealthy foods
Shortage of labor	Food borne illnesses
Lack of land/financing	Obesity/Chronic disease
Unpredictable Weather	Lack of locally grown food
Limited growing season	Expensive inputs
Inhumane animal practices	Poor food storage
Pests	Unsafe food handling
Poor quality foods	Limited market days/hours
High costs of inputs	Distances that foods travel
Environmental impacts	Food deserts
Transition to sustainable practices	Limited purchase power
Lack of awareness/knowledge	Distribution
Waste	Food insecurity
Overhead costs	Inefficiencies
Lack of outreach	Limited markets
Lack of collaboration	Standards not met
Poor economy/lack of jobs	Low yield
Hub, licensed kitchen, incubator, refrigeration	Market failure

Prepare a project budget. Not all funders will support the same expenses. Some will contribute only toward education or training while another may only fund supplies or equipment costs. Be sure to note each funder's **allowable costs**. And check whether the funder wants to see local match (other funds committed or pending for this project.) Project budgets may include these categories:

CATEGORY	DETAIL/QUANTITY	GRANT SHARE	OTHER FUNDING	TOTAL
Personnel	6 hours/week x $10 x 10 weeks	$300	$300	$600
Fringe	15%	$45	$45	$90
Travel	60 miles x 10 weeks x .50	$100	$200	$300
Supplies	6 crates x $50/each	$100	$200	$300
Equipment	1 Scale	$300	$0	$300
Contractual				
Construction				
Other				
Total Expenses		**$845**	**$745**	**$1,590**
% Expenses		**53% Grant**	**47% Match**	**100%**

Some grants will also require a budget justification or narrative explanation as to why each expenses is necessary and reasonable. And a list of other funders and resources being used to carry out the project.

If you are awarded, the funder will expect that the award funding be used to satisfy the funder's purpose and as described in the proposal or application submitted unless the funder is willing to allow slight changes to the plan. Be sure to send a thank you letter to the funder within two weeks of the award. You may wish to ask for their logo and exact wording to be used when publicizing the award on your website or in your newsletter.

You should also be prepared to issue a press release to the media, send a mid-year and a final report discussing the process, inputs, outputs and outcomes. The reports should discuss whether the proposed tasks were completed according to the original proposal, whether the numbers of those who were expected to be impacted were served and whether the anticipated outcomes were achieved. You may also wish to provide the funder with project photos that can be used in their newsletter, webpage and annual report.

If not funded, don't give up. Please know that even excellent proposals may be turned down! Seeking grants is part art, part science and part luck of the draw! A denial can be an opportunity to strengthen the proposal. You may get turned down multiple times before winning an award from a funder. It is worth noting that you or your grant writer cannot control many of the elements that impact giving. Some decision makers may have connections to some of the applicants – including those that build relationships before applying and past awardees who have performed well on past grants by this funder. Some of the other applicants may have had greater need and evidence of that need.

THE DIRECTORY

ACTION FOR HEALTHY KIDS

This organization funds around 400 K-12 schools between $1,000 and $5,000 each year with in-kind contributions in the form of people, programs, and school breakfast and physical activity expertise. Management expertise and support for alternative and universal breakfast or physical activity programs will also be provided. School breakfast program pilots and/or expansions are available for all states while select states are able to apply for the Universal School Breakfast Pilot. See website for application details.
See: www.actionforhealthykids.org/

ADVENTURE CAPITAL

The program's grants are designed to fund student-led wellness projects within the UNITED STATES. Grant amounts and deadlines vary by program. See website for application details.
See: www.school.fueluptoplay60.com/adventure-capital/

THE AETNA FOUNDATION

The Foundation's Regional Grants serve populations who are most at risk for dismal health: low-income, underserved, or minorities. They promote dietary shifts to more fruit and vegetables as well as adding activity to the day. Grants target communities that are in dire need of healthy food purchasing options, as well as places where the society and environment make it difficult for people to be physically active. Projects funded are usually focused on healthy food choices and healthy activity. The Foundation seeks to support schools, communities, economies and gardening/farming efforts. Grants have two levels amounting $25,000 or $50,000. Regional Grants have geographic limitations. See website for application details.
See: www.aetna-foundation.org/foundation/index.html

AGRIBANK

The company's Rural Community Grant Fund is designated for projects and programs in rural communities in western NORTH DAKOTA. Funding is intended to facilitate infrastructure improvement and/or development initiatives encompassing environmental programs, in addition to other areas. Grants of up to $50,000 are available with application deadlines in April, August and November. See website for application details.
See:
www.info.agribank.com/communityinvolvement/rcgf/Pag es/default.aspx

AGRIBUSINESS ASSOCIATION OF KENTUCKY (ABAK)

The Agribusiness Association of Kentucky (ABAK) is an organization established to provide a strong voice in support of KENTUCKY agriculture. ABAK has developed a scholarship program for undergraduate students to help them afford the cost of a post-secondary education. The scholarship program was established in 1996 to recognize and assist Kentucky students majoring in agriculture. The scholarship is in the amount of $1,000 per school year paid in two equal installments of $500 per semester. The scholarship is based on merit as well as financial need. Deadline of April 1st. See website for application details.
See: www.kyagbusiness.org

AGRICULTURE FUTURE OF AMERICA

Agriculture Future of America (AFA) supports academic development through partnerships with rural communities, agriculture organizations, colleges and universities. AFA offers financial support to students who plan to pursue a four-year degree in an agriculture-related field. Currently, AFA offers access to different scholarship programs. A brief description of each program is listed on the web page. See website for application details.

See: www.agfuture.org

AGRI-INNOVATION PROGRAM

The Program is intended to help small to mid-sized businesses with innovative agri-products, technologies or services through the phases of product demonstration and commercialization through 2018 in CANADA. Loans of up to $10 million are available, depending on project type, for for-profit companies or cooperatives in the agricultural industry. See website for application details.

See: www.mentorworks.ca/what-we-offer/government-funding/research-development/aip-stream-b/

AGRI-MARK

The Cooperative offers limited donations and sponsorships to events or organizations focused on community-related causes which are located within the area of the UNITED STATES, where Cabot Creamery and McCadam products are widely available. No deadlines. See website for application details.

See: www.donationsfromthefarmers.coop

AGRI-MARKETING PROGRAM

The Program was created to enhance the marketing capacity and competitiveness of agriculture, agri-food, fish and seafood sectors in CANADA. Support is provided allowing industries to identify market priorities and increase their chances of global success. Up to $1,000,000 is available depending on the Stream of the intended project through 2017.
See: www.mentorworks.ca/what-we-offer/government-funding/business-expansion/agrimarketing/

AGSOUTH FARM CREDIT

The customer-owned cooperative's "Think Outside the Store" campaign awards grants of $500 to community-based farmers markets in GEORGIA and SOUTH CAROLINA for use in advertising and promotion. No deadlines posted. See website for application details.
See: www.agsouthfc.com/news/press-releases/agsouth-encourages-south-carolina-and-georgia-resi.aspx

AGSTAR

The AgStar Fund for Rural America awards grants to organizations in rural communities in WISCONSIN and MINNESOTA that work to improve quality of life through education, technology or the environment. There are several areas of grant-making, including scholarship programs for high school seniors as well as post-secondary education students. See website for application deadlines and grant amounts.
See:
www.agstar.com/enhancingamerica/fundforruralamerica/Pages/default.aspx

AJCC RESEARCH FOUNDATION
The Foundation sponsors competitive research awards annually to fund projects addressing significant issues for the Jersey breed and Jersey milk producers. Awards average $2,000 with an application deadline of December 1st. See website for application details.
See: www.usjersey.com/ResearchFoundation/RFNews_RFP.htm

ALBERTA AGRICULTURAL INITIATIVES PROGRAM
This grant, administered by the Rural Programs branch of ALBERTA, CANADA Agriculture and Food, is intended to improve the quality of life in farming and rural areas of the province. Some communities have used the grant to build community halls, arenas and grandstands, or to support 4-H programs, conferences and festivals. Inquire about using funds toward a Farmers Market or community garden. Agricultural societies and registered non-profit groups may apply. Projects may be funded on a 1:1 cost-share basis. A successful applicant can receive up to $75,000 in grants. No deadlines. See website for application details.
See: www1.agric.gov.ab.ca/general/progserv.nsf/all/pgmsrv61

ALBERTA LOTTERY FUND GRANTS
The Community Initiatives Program (CIP) grants support community programs or services for sports, health, recreation, libraries, arts and culture (may include community garden projects). ALBERTA organizations, such as non-profit charitable groups, municipalities, First Nations groups and Métis Settlements may apply. CIP grants can be used for up to $75,000 and need to be matched by the community, but not always with dollars (volunteer labour, services or donated materials may also be considered). No deadlines. See website for application details.
See: www.culture.alberta.ca/community-and-voluntary-services/community-grants/community-initiatives-program/

ALBERTSONS

The company supports non-profit organizations that wish to provide assistance in the areas of hunger relief, health and nutrition and environmental stewardship. Geographic restrictions apply, deadlines are open. See website for application details.
See: www.albertsons.com/our-company/community-partners/charitable-donations/

ALL THINGS FOOD BOUFFEE 360

The organization provides a list of grants for food-related projects in CANADA.
See: www.allthingsfoodbouffe360.ca/en/resources/gardening-grants-resources-available/

AMERICA IN BLOOM

America in Bloom is an independent, non-profit 501(c)(3) organization dedicated to promoting nationwide beautification programs through the use of flowers, plants, trees, and other environmental lifestyle enhancements. America in Bloom has many community resources including a list of various grant opportunities. See website for application details.
See: www.americainbloom.org/resources/Grant-Opportunities.aspx

AMERICA THE BEAUTIFUL FUND®

America the Beautiful Fund is a national non-profit organization that encourages volunteer citizen efforts and works to protect the natural and historic beauty of America. America the Beautiful Fund is offering grants of free seeds to community groups striving to better our world through gardening. There is a fee for shipping the seeds. See website for application details.
See: www.healthyshasta.org/downloads/gardening/Free-Seeds.pdf

AMERICAN CHESTNUT FOUNDATION

The goal of the American Chestnut Foundation (ACF) is to restore the American Chestnut Tree to our eastern woodlands to benefit our environment, our wildlife, and our society. ACF accepts proposals for its External Grants Program to conduct research concerned with the myriad of aspects involved in chestnut restoration. Research proposal cycles begin in the spring. See website for application details.
See: www.acf.org/external_grants.php

AMERICAN DAIRY SCIENCE ASSOCIATION

The Association's ADSA Awards are intended to recognize ADSA members for outstanding personal achievement. Both students and professionals with the ADSA within the UNITED STATES may nominate themselves or another by January 23rd. See website for application details.
See: www.adsa.org/Membership/ADSAAwards.aspx

AMERICAN FARM BUREAU FOUNDATION FOR AGRICULTURE

The Foundation's Mini-Grant Program funds projects that will increase agricultural literacy. County and State Farm Bureaus may apply for grants of up to $500 for classroom education programs for grades K-12. This foundation also offers White-Reinhardt Teacher Scholarships. Additionally, the National Agriculture in the Classroom Conference Educator Scholarship program provides travel expense funds to educators employed by a school system to attend the national conference and use the information gained to expand their outreach to students regarding food, fiber and fuel. Deadline of October 31st. See website for application details.
See: www.agfoundation.org/

AMERICAN FLORAL ENDOWMENT

The Endowment offers access to research, internships, scholarships and educational programs that promote floriculture and design. The educational grants are due in June. See website for application details.
See: www.endowment.org/grants

AMERICAN HIGHLAND CATTLE ASSOCIATION

The Foundation's grant-making awards organizations with the capacity to contribute to the fulfillment of the HCF's goals of promoting the Highland cattle breed through research and education. The HCF seeks to make grants to organizations where their funds can be "levered" by adding the Highland cattle breed to existing animal study groups in programs with research and educational goals similar to HCF. Application deadlines of December and May 31st. See website for application details.
See: www.highlandcattleusa.org/Default.aspx

THE AMERICAN LAMB BOARD

The American Lamb Board is an industry-funded research and promotions commodity board that represents all sectors of the American Lamb Industry including producers, feeders, seed stock producers, and processors. The Board has two cooperative funding programs available- the Supplier Cooperative Funding Program and the Annual Lamb Promotional Funding Program. The Supplier Cooperative Funding Program is designed for suppliers to help fund branded retail or food service promotions and the Promotional Funding Program is designed for supporting local lamb promotions to help offset the total cost of the promotion. Both programs require a 1:1 cash match from the recipient. Funds for both programs are available twice a year. See: www.lambcheckoff.com/programs-activities/supplier-coop-program/

AMERICAN SEAFOODS COMPANY (ASC)

The ASC organization's community grant program is intended to provide assistance and financial support to ALASKA organizations that are making a real difference in ASC communities addressing issues such as hunger, housing, safety, education, research, or natural resources. Grants range in amount from $500 to $3,000. See website for application details.
See: www.americanseafoodcompany.com

AMERICAN SOYBEAN ASSOCIATION

American Soybean Association is a membership organization that offers award programs including Conservation Legacy Awards and scholarships. The Conservation Legacy Awards program showcases the farm management practices of soybean farmers in the UNITED STATES that are both environmentally friendly and profitable, with winners selected by region. The Secure Optimal Yield (SOY) Scholarship is a $5,000 one-time scholarship ($2,500 per semester) award presented to a high school senior going on to pursue agriculture as an area of study at any accredited college or university. See website for application details.
See: www.soygrowers.com/

AMERICAN VINEYARD FOUNDATION

The American Vineyard Foundation makes grants to improve grape and wine quality, sustainable, address viticulture and enological problems. Submit in January online.
See: http://vit.ucanr.org

AMERICANA FOUNDATION

The Foundation provides support to non-profit organizations, with an emphasis on those operating in MICHIGAN which preserve American agriculture, the conservation of natural resources, and the protection and presentation of expressions of America's heritage. Grant areas include natural resources and agriculture through land use and growth management. Deadlines of January, April, July and October 10th. See website for application details.
See: www.americanafoundation.org/guidelines.asp

RAY C. ANDERSON FOUNDATION

The Foundation was created to promote a sustainable society by supporting and pioneering initiatives that harmonize society, business and the environment. Their mission is achieved through inspiring and funding innovative, educational and project-based initiatives. Grant applications are accepted by invitation only, with funding preference in the Southeast, particularly GEORGIA. See website for details.
See: www.raycandersonfoundation.org/about

ANGUS FOUNDATION

The Foundation is a non-profit organization intended to fund and support programs within the UNITED STATES involving education, youth and research in the Angus breed and the agricultural industry. Undergraduate/Graduate Student Degree Scholarships are also available for students pursuing a degree in higher education. See website for application details.
See: www.angusfoundation.org

ANIMAL WELFARE APPROVED

The program's Grants For Farmers were created to improve animal welfare in farm settings within the UNITED STATES. Funding priorities change every cycle, so check back often to find the category which best suits your project. The program's Good Husbandry Grants are available to those projects which deliver the greatest benefit to farm animals with respect to the amount requested. Grants must be used solely to improve the welfare of farm animals. Only farms currently approved by audit to use the Animal Welfare Approved seals or farms that have an application pending in be in the Animal Welfare Approved program are eligible to apply. Grants amount up to $5,000. Deadline of October 1st. See website for application details.
See: www.animalwelfareapproved.org/farmers/grants-for-farmers/

AMPLE TABLE FOR EVERYONE *(ATE)*

ATE's goal is to identify and fund organizations and individual projects working within the five boroughs of NEW YORK CITY that address at least one of the major obstacles to food security: lack of money, lack of time, limited access to nutritious food, and unfamiliarity with a variety of ingredients, cooking methods and recipes to effect change and engage their communities in meaningful ways that will lead to healthier families.

Two stage application process: submit preliminary proposals by March; qualifying applicants notified in April to submit full applications due early June . Funding decisions in 2015 will be made by August.
See: http://ampletableforeveryone.org/grant-application/

ANNIE'S HOMEGROWN

The company's mission is to cultivate a healthier and happier world by spreading goodness through nourishing foods, honest words and conduct that is considerate and forever kind to the planet. Non-profit organizations and schools may receive small grants for community gardens, school gardens and educational programs for tools, seeds and other supplies, with a December deadline. A scholarship program is also available for full-time undergrad and graduate students studying sustainable agriculture at accredited 2 or 4-year colleges or graduate school in the U.S, with a deadline in January. See: www.annies.com

THE AQUAPONICS ASSOCIATION

The mission is to promote the benefits of aquaponics through education and outreach within the UNITED STATES. The Micro Grant Program was designed for increasing public awareness, understanding and knowledge of aquaponics as an educational tool, a hobby, or a business in providing a source of fresh, local, healthy food. Grants of $1,000 are available to members of the Aquaponics Association quarterly throughout the year. See website for application details.
See: www.aquaponicsassociation.org/micro-grant-program/

ARCHER DANIELS MIDLAND COMPANY (ADM)

The Company's ADM Cares initiative strives to make a positive difference through awarding funds to non-profit organizations that drive meaningful social, economic and environmental progress and promote agricultural development, agricultural education, farm safety or related topics particularly in ADM communities. See website for application details.
See: www.adm.com/en-US/company/CommunityGiving/Pages/default.aspx

THE AUSTIN FOOD & WINE ALLIANCE

The Alliance's Culinary Grant Program is open to food and beverage artisans, producers, culinary professionals and/or those who represent a culinary/food-focused non-profit serving the Austin and/or Central TEXAS community. Grants ranging from $5,000 to $10,000 are awarded in one fiscal year to projects that demonstrate culinary innovation and community giveback and/or support community initiatives. Deadline of October 1st.
See: www.austinfoodwinealliance.org/grants/

THE AWESOME FOUNDATION

The Foundation hopes to create further awesomeness in the universe. Applications for $1,000 micro-grants are accepted on an ongoing, monthly basis.
See: www.awesomefoundation.org

BADGERLAND FINANCIAL

The organization's Beginning with Badgerland grants are designed to assist those in WISCONSIN who have been farming for less than 10 years and wish to farm as a full or part-time vocation. Grants of up to $1,500 are provided to assist with farm business-related expenses. No deadlines..
See: www.badgerlandfinancial.com

JULIA VANDER MAY BAKELAAR CHARITABLE TRUST

The Trust makes grants nationwide for the purposes of supporting education programs for handicapped children, health, human and social service programs run by churches, and community based food programs. Interested applicants should submit a proposal detailing the use of funds and the amount of funding requested. Applicants must be a non-profit organization. Grants of up to $20,000 are available. No application deadline. Write: William Hanse 2035 E. Hamburg Turnpike Wayne, NJ 07470

BANK OF AMERICA CHARITABLE FOUNDATION

The Foundation provides philanthropic support to address needs vital to the health of our communities through addressing basic human services, such as hunger, among other areas. Projects within the UNITED STATES should help provide access to critical food supplies and services to feed individuals, children and families. Past winners have been awarded up to $10,000 for projects such as farm expansions. Deadline of August 8th. See website for program details.See: www.about.bankofamerica.com/en-us/global-impact/charitable-foundation-funding.html#fbid=chYh1ae_Krb

BEEKMAN 1802

Named after an heirloom tomato, the tomato sauce company looks to assist small family farms who have a viable, future focused, growth-oriented business strategy. Applications for their program will be judged on a combination of the feasibility and innovativeness of the applicant's plans, as well as their potential for success. Grants are given in the form of one $10,000 "Lift" and three $1,088 "Mini-Lifts" annually. April deadline. See website for application details. See: www.beekmanmortgagelifter.com

BEN & JERRY'S FOUNDATION'S NATIONAL GRASSROOTS GRANT PROGRAM

The National Grassroots Grant Program offers competitive grants to non-profit, grassroots community organizations with budgets generally under $500,000 in the UNITED STATES, that are working to bring about progressive social change by addressing the underlying conditions of societal and environmental problems. Funding operating and project support, the funding priorities include broad goals that further social justice, protect the environment, and support sustainable food systems. Letters of interest may be submitted online at any time. Grants are for up to $20,000. See: www.benandjerrysfoundation.org/the-grassroots-organizing-for-social-change-program/

FRANK STANLEY BEVERIDGE FOUNDATION (BFF)

The Beveridge Family Foundation exists to fund organizations that serve the common good in Hampden and Hampshire Counties, MASSACHUSETTS. Food, Nutrition and Agriculture programs are among the many causes supported. Grants range from $1,000,000 to $20,000,000. See website for qualification and application details.
See: www.beveridge.org/

BLOOMING PRAIRIE FOUNDATION

The Foundation's purposes are to establish and memorialize the pioneering spirit of Blooming Prairie Cooperative Warehouse in its market area, in the industry, and in the lives of the families who benefited from the products, and the courage and diligence of the people who brought them to market. Applicants must be non-profit organizations working in the areas of development, research, education, promotion and enhancement of organic and natural products, as well as, organizations that are working to promote and enhance the cooperative business model.
See: www.bloomingprairiefoundation.org

BLUE RIDGE WOMEN IN AGRICULTURE

The organization's Mary Boyer Sustainable Food & Agriculture Grant is designed to strengthen the local food system by supporting female farmers, ranchers and processors who want to create innovative, sustainable solutions to production or market obstacles in High Country NORTH CAROLINA or TENNESSEE. Grant applicants should be attempting to complete a sustainable food and agriculture project or pursue educational opportunities related to sustainable food and agriculture. Grants amount $2,000 or less with a deadline of December 19th. Also see the educational and job resources for food producers. See: www.brwia.org/grant-application.html

A.W. BODINE SUNKIST MEMORIAL FUND

Scholarships are awarded to agriculture undergraduate students. Applicants must have financial need and a current family or personal involvement in CALIFORNIA or ARIZONA agriculture. Deadline of April 30th. See: www.sunkist.com/about/bodine_scholarship.aspx

BON APPÉTIT MANAGEMENT COMPANY

Bon Appétit Management Company (BAMC) (not the magazine) is an on-site restaurant company offering full food-service management to corporations, universities, museums, and specialty venues based in Palo Alto, CA and operating more than 500 cafés in 32 states. They have been recognized for their local purchase, Farm to Fork, and cooking from scratch policies and practices. Since 2005, the company has hosted an annual Eat Local Challenge Day during which ten Fork to Farm vendors, two from each of the five geographic regions, are voted to receive grants for under $5,000 to invest in their food, farm or food artisan businesses – such as marketing, hoophouse, fencing, etc. See: www.bamco.com/forktofarm

BONNIE PLANTS
The organization delivers millions of free cabbage plants each year to 3rd grade students in the UNITED STATES. Recipient classrooms have the ability to win a scholarship provided by the organization that totals $1,000 toward education from Bonnie Plants. Teachers of any US 3rd grade classrooms may apply, excluding Alaska and Hawaii. Deadline in February. See website for application details.
See: www.bonniecabbageprogram.com/participate/

OTTO BREMER FOUNDATION
The Foundation gives particular preference to grant-seekers who wish to move their communities forward in meaningful, powerful and broad-based ways. Grants are awarded only to non-profit and government organizations whose beneficiaries are residents of MINNESOTA, NORTH DAKOTA or WISCONSIN, with priority given to local and regional organizations that support Bremer Bank. No deadlines. See:
www.ottobremer.org/grantmaking/grantmaking-overview

BRITISH COLUMBIA MINISTRY OF AGRICULTURE
The Ministry's Growing Forward 2 program offers funding for both farming and food processor businesses in BRITISH COLUMBIA looking to expand or grow. The program funds up to 85% of the cost for an authorized consultant to help develop business plans. Planning can include financial analysis, business development strategies, marketing strategies and other key areas. Program runs through 2018. See website for application details.
See: www.gov.bc.ca/agri/

T.J. BROWN AND C.A. LUPTON FOUNDATION, INC.

The foundation is interested in agriculture and livestock issues and causes, among other areas of interest, primarily in the Fort Worth, Texas area. Non-profits within the UNITED STATES may apply.
Write: PO Box 1629, Fort Worth, TX 76101.

THE BULLITT FOUNDATION

The Foundation's mission is to safeguard the natural environment by promoting responsible human activities and sustainable communities. Funding goes towards environmental issues in urban areas and ecosystem services and planning, among other causes. It serves the Pacific Northwest region including ALASKA, OREGON, WASHINGTON, BRITISH COLUMBIA, IDAHO AND MONTANA. Apply before March and September 15th. See website for application details.
See: www.bullitt.org

BURPEE HOME GARDENS

Burpee Home Gardens promotes home vegetable gardening among young and novice growers through its "I Can Grow" national program, providing awards and supplies to community groups and schools. December deadline. See website for application details.
See: www.burpeehomegardens.com

BUY LOCAL, BUY WISCONSIN

Farmers, individuals, groups, partnerships or businesses in WISCONSIN's food industry may apply for a grant that helps more efficiently process, market and distribute food in local markets to stores, schools and institutions. Applicants must first complete a pre-proposal for the Wisconsin Department of Agriculture, Trade and Consumer Protection (DATCP). The maximum award for each project is $50,000. Grant applicants must provide a cash or in-kind match of at least 50% of the total project budget. Qualified applicants may be involved production agriculture, food processing, food distribution, food warehousing, retail food establishments or agricultural tourism operations. The grants are designed to support local food sales and support the goal of pushing food dollars back into the local economy. Deadline of December 1st. $200,000 in grants will be awarded on an In-Kind basis for the projects. See website for application details.
e: www.datcp.wi.gov/Business/Buy_Local_Buy_Wisconsin /BLBW_Grants/

CALIFORNIA CERTIFIED ORGANIC FOUNDATION

The Foundation supports the education of new organic farmers, ranchers and food processors, in addition to other areas of interest. The Foundation's Future Organic Farmer Grant Fund provides assistance for students in the UNITED STATES pursuing higher or vocational education in organic agriculture. Recipients are judged on having the strongest combination of commitment to leading a lifelong career in organic agriculture, investment and participation in the organic community, and dedication to growing the organic movement. Grants amount to $2,500 to be applied toward their studies. See website for application details.
See: www.ccof.org/press/ccof-foundation-names-recipients-2014-future-organic-farmer-grants

CALIFORNIA FERTILIZER FOUNDATION (CFF)

The California Fertilizer Foundation mission is to enhance awareness of agriculture in CALIFORNIA and its schools. The CFF hosts the School Garden Program to increase the understanding and awareness of agriculture by youth through school gardens. Funding is available to California's public and private elementary, middle and high schools for continuation and/or implementation of in- and after-school garden programs. Grants are $1,200 each. Application deadline of January 15th.
See: www.calfertilizer.org

CALIFORNIA FOUNDATION FOR AGRICULTURE IN THE CLASSROOM

The Foundation's "Look at Agriculture... Organically!" grant program is designed for educators in CALIFORNIA to creatively enhance the understanding of organic agriculture for kindergarten through eighth grade students. Grants up to $1,000 may be used to support the integration of organic agriculture into regular classroom instruction. Deadline of June 13th. See website for application details.
See: www.learnaboutag.org/organicgrants/

CALIFORNIA SEED ASSOCIATION

The California Seed Association is a non-profit trade association. The Association offers scholarships to outstanding students each year who are interested in fields related to Agribusiness. Scholarships amount $2,500 each with an application deadline of February 1st. See website for application details.
See: www.calseed.org/scholarship.html

CALIFORNIA STRAWBERRY COMMISSION

The organization's Scholarship Program was founded by farmers to enable children of strawberry farm workers to further their educational and career goals. The scholarship is for graduating high school seniors with continuing funding available. Eligible students must have at least one parent who is currently employed and has been employed in the past two consecutive seasons in the CALIFORNIA strawberry harvest. Scholarships start at $400 and are applied toward full-time status at a four-year college or university, community college or accredited trade school. Applications are due by March 1st of each year. See website for application details.
See: www.californiastrawberries.com

DAVE CAMERON EDUCATIONAL FOUNDATION

The Foundation awards scholarships of between $500 and $2,000 to agricultural students from the York, SOUTH CAROLINA area.
Write: PO Box 181, York, South Carolina 29745

4H CANADA

The organization provides a list of grants, scholarships and awards for 4H clubs and members in CANADA.
See: www.apply.4-h-canada.ca/

CANADA BUSINESS NETWORK

The Network lists opportunities for businesses in CANADA to receive public funds to help springboard their business ventures.
See: www.canadabusiness.ca/eng/page/2740/

CANADA BUSINESS ONTARIO
The organization provides a guide for agricultural businesses in ONTARIO who need financing tools and programs to offset the cost of doing business.
See: www.cbo-eco.ca/en/index.cfm/financing/government-loans-and-grants/grants-subsidies-and-contributions-agriculture/

CANADIAN ORGANIC GROWERS
The Canadian Organic Growers (COG) was founded in 1975 to promote organic growing in order to build healthy local communities and ecosystems. As the largest organic association in CANADA, with members in every province and one territory, COG works to develop the organic sector by encouraging farmers to transition to organic methods, by creating consumer awareness through public education campaigns, and, by encouraging governments to develop policies to support food organic systems.
See: www.cog.ca

THE CAPTAIN PLANET FOUNDATION
The Foundation provides grants to non-profit organizations and schools, mostly within the UNITED STATES, who promote and support high-quality educational programs that enable youth to understand and appreciate our world through learning experiences that engage them in active, hands-on projects to improve the environment. Grants up to $2,500; deadlines in the fall and winter. Special grants are also available for STEM fields that use innovation, biomimicry/nature-based design, with sustainable solutions, or new uses for technology to address environmental problems in our communities. See:
www.captainplanetfoundation.org

CAROLYN FOUNDATION

The Carolyn Foundation has a vision is to improve the lives of children/families, communities and the environment. The foundation offers Community Development grants in New Haven, CONNECTICUT and Minneapolis, MINNESOTA. Environmental grants in the Upper Midwest five state area (ND, SD, MN, WI, IA) with a focus on sustainability, community action, and other activities that mitigate climate change. Online deadlines of February 1st and August 1st. Most environmental grant awards are $15,000 to $30,000. See website for application details. See: www.carolynfoundation.org

THE CARROT PROJECT

The organization offers financing to farm, forestry and fishery businesses as well as food system enterprises within the GREATER BERKSHIRES, MAINE, MASSACHUSETTS and VERMONT. Loan terms and information vary depending on the area. Loans amount from $5,000 to $50,000 on average. No deadlines. See: www.thecarrotproject.org/financing

CCOF Foundation

The Foundation is working with the UNFI Foundation, Driscoll's, the National Cooperative Grocers Association and the Clif Bar Family Foundation to provide grants to teachers and students in the UNITED STATES. K-8 grade and higher and vocational education applications open April 10th, with a due date of May 15th, 2015. High school grants made through Future Farmers of America open in September with a closing date in November. The grants range from $1,000 to $2,500 for students to study organic agriculture nationally. See website for application details. See: www.ccof.org/ccof/structure/ccof-foundation/future-organic-farmer-grant-fund

CEDAR TREE FOUNDATION

The Foundation supports sustainable agriculture and environmental health among other causes, primarily in NEW YORK, with some giving nationally. Particular consideration is given to proposals that demonstrate strong elements of environmental justice and conservation. Letters of inquiry are accepted on a rolling basis from non-profit organizations within the UNITED STATES. There is no deadline. Grants average around $4,000. See website for application details.
See: www.cedartreefound.org

THE CERES TRUST

The Trust's mission is to support and promote organic and sustainable agriculture. The Trust's grants support research in organic agriculture at universities and to graduate students, education to create careers in the production and processing of certified organic food, programs to eliminate pesticide exposure and GMO contamination, and efforts to preserve crop biodiversity and public access to seeds. There are several grant areas with varying deadlines, geographic restrictions and amounts available. See website for program areas and application details.
See: www.cerestrust.org/

THE HARRY CHAPIN FOUNDATION

The Harry Chapin Foundation supports non-profit organizations within the UNITED STATES that have demonstrated an ability in helping people to become self-sufficient and ultimately improve people lives, with an emphasis on Agricultural and Environmental programs, among other areas of interest. The funds average from $300-$10,000, with no application deadlines. See website for application details.
See: www.harrychapinfoundation.org/

THE CHARTER ONE FOUNDATION
The Foundation's Charter One Growing Communities program awards grants of up to $3,000 to emerging local businesses or farmers involved in Detroit, MICHIGAN's food sector. Grants are meant to fund what the food-based operations need to further their business within the community. Deadline of July 25th.
See: www.detroiteasternmarket.com/

CHIPOTLE CULTIVATE FOUNDATION
The Foundation's grant-making focuses on assisting family farms who are committed to sustainable farming practices, organizations that are working to develop an affordable, sustainable pasture-based system of animal production, and organizations promoting better food through innovation or education. Applications are accepted by invitation only, but organizations are welcome to contact the Foundation with information about programs and projects that fall within their funding areas. December deadlines.
See: www.cultivatefoundation.org

CHS FOUNDATION
Supports education & leadership projects that invest in agriculture, cooperative business and rural America. There are various grant opportunities with varying deadlines and amounts available. See website for application details.
See: www.chsinc.com

CLEAN ENERGY FINANCE AND INVESTMENT AUTHORITY
The Authority's Anaerobic Digestion Pilot Program is designed for most commercial, industrial and institutional businesses in CONNECTICUT which produce large volumes of organic waste and/or have high power loads. Funding will not exceed the equivalent of $450/kilowatt generated. Deadline of February 27th. See: www.energizect.com/businesses/programs/Anaerobic-Digester-Projects

CLIF BAR FAMILY FOUNDATION

The Foundation's Small Grants program awards grants averaging $8,000 to non-profit organizations in the UNITED STATES that are working to strengthen local food systems and communities, enhance public health, and safeguard the environment and natural resources in a select number of states. Quarterly deadlines. See website for application information.
See: www.clifbarfamilyfoundation.org/Grants-Programs

CLIMATE, FOOD AND FARMING RESEARCH NETWORK

The Network provides funding to students from developing countries who are currently enrolled in PhD programs to apply for short-term scientific training and research stays at CGIAR research centers. Applicants should have a background in agriculture and climate change research, as well as a interest in mitigation of greenhouse gas emissions from agriculture. Students with experience in crop-livestock systems are especially sought. Grants of up to $10,000 are available for stays between 3 and 4 months. Deadline of September 30th. See website for application details.
See: www.ccafs.cgiar.org/

COLORADO GARDEN FOUNDATION

The organization supports horticulture and horticultural related projects and those groups that are involved or directly related in COLORADO. Education is emphasized. Areas of interest include horticultural-related research, education, therapy and community improvements. Grants $300 to $15,000.
See: www.coloradogardenfoundation.org/grants

COLORADO STATE UNIVERSITY

The University's High Plains Intermountain Center for Agricultural Health & Safety is offering Pilot Grants for innovative researchers within the University to conduct projects that promote worker health and safety in agriculture, forestry, or fishing. Grants amount up to $25,000. Deadline of August 15th. See website for application details.
See: www.csu-cvmbs.colostate.edu/academics/erhs/agricultural-health-and-safety/Pages/pilot-grants.aspx

COMMUNITY C.R.O.P.S.

The staff and volunteers at Community C.R.O.P.S. work hard for families who are able to grow food for themselves and the market. Community C.R.O.P.S. (Combining Resources, Opportunities, and People for Sustainability) helps people work together to grow healthy food and live sustainability, funds many community gardens and provides farming training and offers scholarships to participants with limited resources to attend workshops. Community C.R.O.P.S. also offers both summer and winter classes for the prospective farmer.
See: www.communitycrops.org/farm

COMMUNITY FARMS PROGRAMS

The organization lists grant/loans for new and seasoned farmers in CANADA.
See:
www.communityfarms.ca/resources/grantsLoans.shtml

COMMUNITY FOOD CO-OP

The Community Food Co-op of Bellingham, WASHINGTON offers Farm Fund grants to support projects in Whatcom County that strengthen local, sustainable farms and the local food system. Deadline in January. See: www.communityfood.coop/participate/giving-back/farm-fund/

COMMUNITY FOUNDATION OF FREDERICK COUNTY

The Foundation awards grants annually to Frederick County, MARYLAND residents who create positive and lasting impact. Grant areas include environmental causes, among other areas of interest. Grant-making varies by focus, deadline and amount, so check website often for update. See: www.cffredco.org/receive/grants

THE COMMUNITY FOUNDATIONS OF THE HUDSON VALLEY

The Hudson Valley Farm Fresh Food grant program gives up to $25,000 to non-profit organizations in Dutchess, Ulster and Putnam Counties NEW YORK who strive to increase access to local, farm fresh food for individuals who are considered food insecure. Organizations involved in growing, collecting, distributing and serving farm fresh food and meals to those in need; including Community Supported Agriculture (CSA's), agricultural and nutritional educational organizations, food pantries, soup kitchens, shelters and other nonprofit organizations are encouraged to submit a letter of inquiry. Applications due in March. See: www.cfhvny.org

CONAGRA FOODS FOUNDATION

Beginning again in December 2015, non-profit charitable organizations can apply for the Foundation's Community Impact Grants program that makes awards to "impactful, grassroots organizations that leverage innovation and creativity to address child hunger and nutrition" in communities where ConAgra Food's employees live and work (AR, CA, GA, ID, IL, MI, MO, OR, TN & WA), and, where food insecurity rates among children are significant. Begin by downloading the guidelines (which can vary year to year), ensuring eligibility, and completing an online letter of inquiry. Grants ranges from $10,000 to $75,000.
See: www.conagrafoods.com/our-company/our-commitment/foundation

CONNECTICUT DEPARTMENT OF AGRICULTURE

The organization's Farm Transition Grant Program was designed to support activity which promotes agriculture stability and/or increases the economic viability of farm business by matching funds of CONNECTICUT farmers and agricultural cooperatives. Producers and coops may apply with awards up to $49,999 in matching funds in November.
See: www.ct.gov/doag/cwp/view.asp?a=3260&q=419410

CONSERVATION, FOOD & HEALTH FOUNDATION

The Foundation promotes the conservation of natural resources, improve the production and distribution of food, and improve health in the developing world and helps build capacity within developing countries in the areas of conservation, food, and health with grants for special projects and programs of non-governmental organizations. The Foundation prefers to support organizations located in or whose activities are of direct and immediate benefit to developing countries. Grants range in amount from $17,000 to $25,000. No deadlines. .
See: www.cfhfoundation.grantsmanagement08.com/

CONSTELLATION ENERGY

The company's Community Champions program awards grants to causes that improve communities. Grants of up to $500 are awarded to non-profit organizations with up to $250 for other community causes. No deadlines. See website for application details.
See: www.constellation.com/community/pages/community-champions.aspx

THE CONSUMER WELLNESS CENTER

The Center is a non-profit organization dedicated to promoting nutrition as a way to prevent disease and enhance human health and longevity. Their Nutrition Education Grant Program offers $1,000 grants to people and organizations in the UNITED STATES. Deadline of November 25th. See:
www.consumerwellness.org/PR22.html

COULEE FOOD SYSTEM COALITION

The Coalition is committed to building a food system that is healthy, ecologically sustainable, economically vibrant, culturally relevant and socially just. Its Food For All grants funds programs, activities, and projects that benefit a population within the boundaries of La Crosse County, WISCONSIN. Grants typically amount around $5,000. Application deadline of September 15th. Application information can be found online.
See: www.couleefoodsystem.org

COUNTRY VISIONS COOPERATIVE
The company's scholarship program is intended for graduating high school seniors moving on to a post-secondary education. Ten $1,000 scholarships are for WISCONSIN and MICHIGAN students whose parents, parent or legal guardian is a member of Country Visions Coop and has purchased at least $2,000 worth of goods and services in the prior year. Deadline of March 31st. See website for application details.
See: www.countryvisionscoop.com

THE JAMES COX FOUNDATION
The James M. Cox Foundation provides community support in several areas, including: conservation and environment, early childhood education, empowering families and individuals for success, and health in communities NATIONWIDE where Cox Enterprises or its subsidiaries operate. It recently made a sizeable gift to Georgia Organics to support Farm to School efforts. Federally tax exempt nonprofits or equipment government agencies may apply for capital funding or special projects. Must have an endorsement letter from an area Cox business leader. Online applications only.
See: http://www.coxenterprises.com/corporate-responsibility/giving/foundations.aspx

CROPP COOPERATIVE'S FAFO FUND

The organic farmers of the CROPP Cooperative, producers for Organic Valley® and Organic Prairie® products contribute to the Farmers Advocating for Organics (FAFO) fund each year. A committee of CROPP farmers reviews proposals from individuals and organizations seeking funding for particular projects or programs dedicated to furthering organic education, organic farming or product research, and organic advocacy and decides how to distribute the funds. There is no deadline for grants less than $5,000; the deadline for larger requests is in September. See website for application details.
See: www.organicvalley.coop/about-us/donations/fafo-fund/

C.S. FUND

The CS Fund and Warsh/Mott Legacy are private foundations that are dedicated to progressive social change with food sovereignty being an area of interest, among others. Grant-seekers must be non-profits organizations, with a majority of grants awarded being given within the UNITED STATES. No deadlines. See website for application information.
See www.csfund.org/seekingagrant.html

THE CULINARY TRUST

The Trust's "Growing Leaders Fund" is designed for innovative culinary professionals in philanthropic, social entrepreneurship and small business arenas who wish to address critical issues in food. The Fund will provide tools and opportunities to individuals or organizations who are focused on the culinary industry or food-related programming. Grants of up to $5,000 are provided year round. See website for application details.
See: www.theculinarytrust.org/growing-leaders-fund/

DAIRY FARMERS OF AMERICA

The organization awards scholarships to incoming freshmen, undergraduate students, and graduate/professional students in the UNITED STATES who are pursuing a career in the dairy industry or related field. Deadline of January 15th. See website for application details.
See: www.dfamilk.com/careers/scholarships

DAIRY SPOT

The organization hopes to fund local grassroots dairy promotion programs or events geared towards consumers. Events should focus on promotion of the dairy industry on a local level, with the consumer's wants and needs in mind. Applicants must be a dairy farmer in the Mid-Atlantic Dairy Association and Pennsylvania Dairy Promotion Program service territory. 25 grants of $250 will be awarded throughout the year.
See: www.dairyspot.com

THE DANNON COMPANY, INC.

The company strives to facilitate change for a positive future. Non-profit organizations within 60 miles of a Dannon facility location: Salt Lake City, UTAH; Fort Worth, TEXAS; White Plains, NEW YORK; and Minster, OHIO are eligible to apply for a grant. Preference is given to projects which champion Dannon's mission to bring health through their products to the greatest number of people. Grants amount up to $5,000. Applications are accepted year-round. See website for application details.
See: www.dannon.com/dannon-cares/

DAUGHTERS OF AMERICAN AGRICULTURE (DAA)

The DAA Foundation provides $1,000 scholarships to farm, ranch and agribusiness women or their daughters in two categories: the Jean Ibendahl scholarship to high school graduates age 18-23 and the Sister Thomas More Bertels scholarship to women age 24 and over. Scholarship funds may be used for accredited courses in agricultural leadership, communications, rural sociology, medicine, or other courses directly related to agriculture. Dues June 1. See: www.americanagriwomen.org

DEAN FOODS FOUNDATION

The Foundation supports organizations and programs that ensure children have access to the healthy foods they need to grow and thrive, as well as opportunities to engage in youth leadership programs. Childhood Nutrition, Youth Leadership and Dairy Stewardship are areas of interest, among other pursuits. Non-profit organizations, or those sponsored by a non-profit within the UNITED STATES may apply for funding in the spring and fallSee: www.responsibility.deanfoods.com

JOHN DEERE FOUNDATION

The Foundation awards grants to non-profit organizations who are working to provide change and betterment within the areas of world hunger, education and community development. They give to locations within the UNITED STATES which are nearest the major John Deere operating units, select areas of CANADA and internationally. There is a variety of grants to with varying deadlines and amounts. Giving primarily in areas of corporation operations – GA, IA, IL, KS, WI, LA, MO, NC, ND, and TN. Agriculture is among causes. Application form required. See: www.deere.com

THE DEPARTMENT OF ENVIRONMENTAL MANAGEMENT OF RHODE ISLAND

The Department's grant funding is intended to enhance the competitiveness of specialty crops grown in RHODE ISLAND. Agricultural or educational associations or organizations, farmers and/or Rhode Island residents are eligible to apply for funding. Grants range in amount from $10,000 to $50,000 and are awarded half up front and half upon completion of the intended project with an application deadline of Match 31st. See website for application details.
See: www.rigrown.ri.gov

GERALDINE R. DODGE FOUNDATION

Awards grants in NEW JERSEY to promote and achieve ecosystem resilience and environmentally healthy, sustainable communities, connect people to their natural world, and, build an environmental ethic of care and responsibility. Preference is given to non-profit organizations that: Increase the quality, function and public accessibility of watersheds through land preservation, resource management, and stewardship; Focus on urban greening, particularly through community-led design and decision making and Help develop regional food systems, including rural-to-urban farming connections and urban food market development. November and August deadlines.
See: www.grdodge.org

DONORS CHOOSE

Teachers submit project ideas to the website and are sponsored by individuals who support their ideas. Amounts given vary and deadlines are open.
See: www.donorschoose.org

DRISCOLL'S

The company's Community Grants Program support solutions that build vibrant communities with a new level of understanding, partnerships, economic growth, and innovation between agriculture and the communities. Grants are awarded to non-profit organizations located within regional areas of interest, as well as to pre-selected non-profit groups who have been invited to submit proposals. See website for application details.
See: www.driscolls.com

DUPONT PIONEER

The company's Curriculum for Agricultural Science Education (CASE) program works with the National Association of Agricultural Educators to award $2,500 to $5,000 grants to teachers who are implementing CASE in the classroom – offering training, equipment and resources to prepare students for careers in agriculture/food. Deadline October 30th. CASE Institute Scholarships are also available. Also DuPont Pioneer's Giving Program provides up to $5,000 for a project that focuses on: PreK-12 education (e.g., support of science fairs, teaching gardens and greenhouses, local FFA and 4H programs), community betterment, and food security (e.g., home backpack meal programs, food banks, rural and congregate meal programs, meals on wheels programs, community gardens).
See: www.case4learning.org/index.php/professional-development/scholarships-grants or pioneer.com

EVERGREEN

Evergreen, a non-profit that works to make cities more liveable and empowers Canadians to deepen the connection with nature, offers grants through its Green Grants program. Walmart Canada and Evergreen combined efforts to offer funding to community-based initiatives across CANADA for a number of green projects including community food gardens along with other initiatives. Community groups and non-profit organizations working on community development and environmental initiatives in underserved communities can apply for up to $10,000 (up to 50% of project budget). Cost items range from supplies to tools to wages. February deadline. Also see Evergreen's website for a list of other funders for green projects. See: www.evergreen.ca/get-involved/funding-opportunities/green-grants/

FAIR FOOD NETWORK

The national nonprofit organization, dedicated to growing the good for a more just and sustainable food system, developed the Double Up Food Bucks - MICHIGAN's statewide healthy food incentive program that increases access to healthy food for low-income Americans and puts more money in the pockets of family farmers. See: fairfoodnetwork.org and doubleupfoodbucks.org.

FARM AID

Farm Aid works throughout the year to build a thriving family farm-centered system of agriculture. They fund family farm and rural service organizations to keep family farmers on the land producing good food for all. Non-profit organizations within the UNITED STATES may apply before August 1st. Grants range in amount from $3,000 to $10,000. See:
www.farmaid.org/site/c.qlI5IhNVJsE/b.2723621/k.9C20/Grant_Program.htm

FARM CREDIT EAST

The organization's AgEnhancement Program helps organizations promote awareness of agriculture in NEW ENGLAND, NEW YORK and NEW JERSEY. Eligible organizations promote and strengthen the agriculture, forest products or commercial fishing industries in the region. Applications due by April, August and December 1st. Grants from $500 to $8,000. See:
www.farmcrediteast.com

FARM CREDIT SERVICES OF AMERICA

The organization's Working Here Fund awards grants to projects and organizations that make a positive, long-term impact in IOWA, NEBRASKA, SOUTH DAKOTA and WYOMING, in the areas of agriculture education, young and beginning producers and hunger and nutrition. Grants $2,000 each. Deadline of December 31st. Apply online. See:
www.fcsamerica.com/contact/grant-program/grant-program-information

FARM FOLK CITY FOLK

The organization, with cooperation from the Island Chef's Collaborative and Vancity, offers micro loans to local food producers within Metro VANCOUVER, the SUNSHINE COAST, FRASER VALLEY, VANCOUVER ISLAND and the GULF ISLANDS in CANADA. The aim is to provide capital for farmers, fishers, ranchers, harvesters and processors to invest in equipment and materials that allows them to increase the supply of local food in their region. Loans range from $1,000 to $10,000 with +4% interest for 24 month term. See:
www.farmfolkcityfolk.ca/resources/microloan/

FARMSTART

The organization provides a list of loans and grants for young and beginning farmers and farm transfers in CANADA. See:
www.farmstart.ca/provincial-measures-specifically-targeting-young-and-beginning-farmers-and-farm-transfers/

FARM TO SCHOOL GRANT PROGRAM

The program's initiative is to improve access to local foods within eligible schools. Grants are awarded for training, supporting operations, planning, purchasing equipment, developing school gardens, developing partnerships, and implementing farm to school programs. Grant amounts depend on the category of the project. Eligible schools, state and local agencies, Indian tribal organizations, agricultural producers or groups of agricultural producers and non-profit entities may apply. School eligibility requirements can be found on the website. See: www.fns.usda.gov/farmtoschool/farm-school-grant-program, and http://www.farmtoschool.org/resources for even more opportunities!

FARMER VETERAN COALITION

The Coalition works with veterans in the food and farming community within the UNITED STATES to provide farming education and veteran assistance to those in need. Their Farming Fellowship program assists veterans with advancing their careers in food and farming. Participants are given access to resources and support services that enable them to become successful in the food and farming industry. Grants of $2,500 to $5,000 are awarded to veteran farmers for the tools they need to grow and manage sustainable farms. Grantees are also offered in-kind supplies, farming education and one-on-one farming advice and mentorship. See website for application details.
See: www.farmvetco.org

FARMS AT WORK

The organization provides a list of farm-related grant opportunities in CANADA.
See: www.farmsatwork.ca/Grant_opportunities

FIRST FRUITS OF WASHINGTON

First Fruits of Washington, an initiative of WASHINGTON fruit growers Broetje Orchards, offers financial help to low income first generation college students. Vista Hermosa Foundation is the charitable arm of Broetje Orchards – addressing rural communities and immigration among other causes. There are three types of scholarships available including First Fruits scholarships, Continuing Education scholarships, and the Adult Lifetime Learning scholarship. Grant amounts vary. Applications are reviewed biannually.
See: www.firstfruits.com/scholarships.html

FIRST MID-ILLINOIS BANK & TRUST

Scholarships to Coles County ILLINOIS students pursuing a career in an agriculture field. April 15th deadline. Write: Scholarships, First Mid-Illinois Bank & Trust, PO Box 499 Mattoon Illinois 61938-0499

FIRST NATIONS

Through the Institute's Native Agriculture and Food Systems Initiative, investments into innovative institutions and models are made whose goals include strengthening asset control and economic development support for American Indian people and their communities. Grants range from $20,000 to $25,000 and support projects that increase access to fresh, healthy foods. Priority will be given to projects which increase the availability of healthy, locally produced foods in Native communities as well as projects that work to reduce food insecurity and entrepreneurship programs that create systemic change by increasing community control of local food systems. Eligible parties include Native American-controlled nonprofit tribal organizations and community-based groups with healthy food access goals. March deadline.
See: www.firstnations.org/NAFSI

FIRST THINGS FIRST

The organization's grant program awards funding to non-profit, government, Tribal, higher learning and private organizations, providing services in ARIZONA which address the specific development and health needs for children birth through age five, and their families. Varying grants, with varying deadlines may be accessed via the organization's website when available.
See: www.azftf.gov/WhatWeDo/Funding/Pages/Eligibility.aspx

FISKARS® PROJECT ORANGE THUMB®

The Fiskars® Project Orange Thumb® grant program is intended to recognize projects within the UNITED STATES and CANADA that will make differences in their communities through unique community garden initiatives while demonstrating and communicating how a small group of people can make changes that affect and involve the entire community. The grant program "sowing the seeds of community change" makes awards valued at $5,000 (combination of cash and Fiskars® items to help support the goals of neighborhood beautification and horticulture education). Applications accepted from non-profit organizations from late September to early December. See website for application details.
See: www2.fiskars.com/Community/Project-Orange-Thumb/

FLORIDA AG IN THE CLASSROOM

The program distributes Teacher Grants to general education K-12 teachers and agri-science teachers in FLORIDA who have agriculture related classroom or schoolyard projects they would like to carry out. Additionally, grants are available for educators who wish to start or add on to a school garden. Grants of $500 are available. See website for application details.
See: www.faitc.org/grants/

FLORIDA STRAWBERRY GROWERS ASSOCIATION
The Florida Strawberry Growers Association is a membership association that offers scholarships including an Ambassador scholarship to encourage young men and women to continue their education beyond high school. The scholarship will be no less than $500. Applications must be postmarked and completed by September 1st. See website for application details.
See: www.flastrawberry.com/education/scholarships/

FOOD AND FARM COMMUNICATIONS FUND
The Fund was created to expand the "Good Food Movement's" communications capacity. Grants are awarded by the Fund against a specific set of goals and outcomes to non-profit organizations within the UNITED STATES. Grants range in amount from $10,000 to $100,000. Letters of Inquiry must be received by July 1st. See website for application details.
See: www.foodandfarmcommunications.org/about.html

FOOD ANIMAL CONCERNS TRUST
The Trust's Fund-a-Farmer Project is designed to empower family farmers to positively impact farm animal welfare. Grants are awarded for projects within the UNITED STATES that help family farmers transition to pasture-based systems, improve the marketing of their humane products, or to generally enrich the conditions in which their farm animals are raised. The organization will award grants of between $500 and $1,500. To be eligible, farms must raise at least one of the following animal species: pigs, broiler chickens, laying hens, dairy cows, and/or beef cattle. Grants will be made only to farmers for a project on a working, independent family farm. November deadline. See:
www.foodanimalconcerns.org

FOOD CO-OP INITIATIVE

The Food Co-op Initiative Program seeks to enable a faster and more efficient start-up process to develop new retail grocery co-ops. The Seed Fund, when funding is available, provides early development capital of up to $10,000 to co-op organizing groups within the UNITED STATES in the form of 1:1 matching funds. Applicants must intend on becoming a cooperative organization and fully understand the cooperative structure, values and principles. The Sprout Fund provides capital during the mid to later stages of planning and implementation by incorporated cooperative organizations. Loans up to $25,000 and must be matched in equal dollars by the cooperative. Download the applications. See: www.foodcoopinitiative.coop/resources/loans

FOOD FOR THOUGHT ENDOWMENT FUND, INC.

The fund makes scholarship awards to students within the UNITED STATES pursuing education related to the food industry. Applications should include the applicant's vision of the future of the food industry and the role he/she contemplates playing in it through his/her career choice. Deadline in March.
Write: Food Industry Alliance of NYS, Inc., 130 Washington Avenue, Albany NY 12210

FOUNDATION FOR AGRICULTURE

The Foundation is designed to fund projects in the UNITED STAES that will increase agricultural literacy. County and state Farm Bureaus may apply for grants of up to $500 for classroom education programs for grades K-12 in order to initiate new ag literacy programs or expand existing programs to additional grades levels or new subject areas. Two grant cycles with deadlines in October and April. Apply online. See:
www.agfoundation.org/index.php?action=whatwesupport.minigrants

FOUNDATION FOR RURAL SERVICE

The Foundation aims to aid non-profit organizations within the UNITED STATES that build and sustain a high quality of life for rural communities. Grants are intended to allow rural communities to take the first step towards a project or plan that can help better the lives of those around them. Grant categories include business development, community development, education and telecommunications. Priority will be given to projects that could be fully funded by the grant maximum of $5,000 or have 75% or more of the project currently funded. Grant amounts range from $250 to $5,000. See website for application details.
See: www.frs.org/rural-community-outreach/grant-program

FRONTERA FARMER FOUNDATION

The Frontera Farmer Foundation, founded by the proprietors of Frontera® Grill and Topolobampo, was created out of concern for struggling farmers and the importance of local produce to the vitality of Chicago's culinary culture. The Foundation is committed to small sustainable Midwestern farms who are more likely to promote biodiversity by planting a wide range of produce and operate using organic practices with grants for capital improvements of up to $12,000 to small and medium sized individually owned farms that sell their food products to customers in the Chicago, ILLINOIS area at farmers markets and otherwise. March 1st deadline. See website for application details.
See: www.rickbayless.com/foundation

THE FRUITGUYS COMMUNITY FUND
The Fund's mission aims to support farms, farmers, non-profits and policies that allow for greater environmental and economic health, community engagement and advocacy that embrace sustainable practices. Grants typically range in amount from $3,500 to $5,000. Deadline in February.
See: www.fruitguyscommunityfund.org

FRUIT TREE PLANTING FOUNDATION
The Foundation is dedicated to planting fruitful trees and plants to alleviate world hunger, combat global warming, strengthen communities and improve the surrounding air, soil and water. Orchard donations are available to non-profit organizations, public or non-profit schools and government entities who pledge to care for the trees and utilize them for a charitable purpose. Applicants must own the planting site or have long-term arrangements to remain at the site, be committed to caring for the trees, have a source of irrigation nearby and can help coordinate local volunteers to join in on the day of planting. No deadline.
See: www.ftpf.org

FUEL UP TO PLAY 60
This initiative encourages K-12 schools within the UNITED STATES to apply for up to $4,000 per year to improve healthy eating and physical activity opportunities within their school. Applicants must be enrolled in the Fuel Up to Play 60 national program. Deadlines change with school calendar years. See website for current grant offerings and application details.
See: www.school.fueluptoplay60.com/home.php

FUTURE FARMERS OF AMERICA

National Future Farmers of America organization offer Grants and Scholarships to farmers for the next generation. The mission is to promote farming and community involvement through lesson plans and service learning. Grants are awarded toward project costs that emphasize community involvement in rural communities. The grants program is aimed to address world hunger problems and to promote leadership opportunities in rural communities. See website for application details.
See: www.ffa.org/programs/grantsandscholarships/Pages/default.aspx#

GARDEN ABCs

The organization lists funding opportunities for youth and community garden-related projects within the UNITED STATES on their website.
See: www.gardenabcs.com/grants.html

THE GARDEN CLUB OF AMERICA

The Garden Club of America provides scholarships and awards for visionary student leaders and educators. 27 merit-based scholarships are awarded each year in a variety of areas of study. See website for application details.
See: www.gcamerica.org

THE GARDEN CLUB OF BUZZARDS BAY

The mission of the Garden Club of Buzzards Bay is to stimulate the knowledge and love of gardening through education in development of gardens, their design, management and culture and to restore, improve and protect the environment through education, programs and activities in the field of conservation, horticulture and civic improvement. The Club awards grants to non-profits in the coastal area of MASSACHUSETTS for projects promoting civic beautification, conservation, community garden programs at schools and sustainable agriculture projects. February deadline. See website for application details.
See: www.gardenclubbuzzardsbay.org

GARDENS TO HOSPITALS

The organization's grant program seeks to help medical facilities nationwide build edible, organic gardens for serving their patients, staff and community. Grants are awarded to hospitals and medical facilities interested in building and/or expanding an edible, organic garden. Each hospital will have the option to enlist the help of a farm coach who will aid in the organic certification process and provide sustainable practices for the long-term resilience of the garden. Grant deadline in the fall.
See: www.gardenstohospitals.org

GLIDE FOUNDATION

The Foundation supports non-profit organizations within the UNITED STATES which are committed to agricultural and preservation of land, among other pursuits. Applicants may request funding for capital acquisition and renovation projects. Grants amount up to $50,000. Deadline of August 15th. Applications are available online.
See: www.glidefoundation.org/grants/

THE FRED C. GLOECKNER FOUNDATION, INC.

The Fred C. Gloeckner Foundation awards grants for research and educational projects in floriculture and related fields at universities, colleges and Federal research institutions within the UNITED STATES. Grants are awarded on the basis of project outlines, including objectives as well as methods, procedures, materials, equipment are considered when support by a research project online. Applications must be postmarked before April 1st. See website for application details.
See: www.gloecknerfoundation.org/fundingp.htm

GOLDEN LEAF FOUNDATION

The Foundation's Open Grants Program strives to strengthen NORTH CAROLINA's long-term economy, especially in tobacco-dependent, economically distressed, and/or rural communities by focusing on agriculture, among other areas. Governmental entities and non-profits may apply with projects in areas such as value-added processing, market expansion, and alternative crops, livestock and aquaculture. Applications accepted on a rolling basis.
See: www.goldenleaf.org

GOOD FOOD AWARDS

The Good Food Awards celebrate tasty, authentic and responsibly produced foods by American producers and the farmers who share their ingredients. Awards are given to winners in 11 categories: beer, charcuterie, cheese, chocolate, coffee, confections, pickles, preserve, spirits, oil and honey. Awards are given to producers and their food communities from each of five regions of the US.
See: www.goodfoodawards.org

GREENBELT FUND
The Greenbelt Fund supports and enhances the viability, integrity, and sustainability of agriculture in ONTARIO and Ontario's Greenbelt. The Fund delivers support to farmers and local food leaders to ensure more of the good things that grow in Ontario are being served and distributed through our public institutions, retail and food service markets. Two grant streams included are Broader Public Sector Grants and Market Access Grants. See website for application details.
See: www.greenbeltfund.ca

GREEN EDUCATION FUND
The Fund is committed to creating a sustainable future through education. The Fund provides curriculum and resources to K-12 students and teachers worldwide with the goal of challenging them to think holistically and critically about global environmental concerns and solutions. There are a variety of grants awarded, with different amounts and deadlines available. See website for application details.
See: www.greeneducationfoundation.org

GROWMARK
GROWMARK and participating FS member cooperatives make scholarships available to active high-school FFA members in ILLINOIS, IOWA, and WISCONSIN through an essay contest where participants learn more about agriculture and cooperatives. Another contest is available to high school FFA members in ONTARIO. See website for application details.
See: www.growmark.com/OurCommitments/Pages/Youth -and-Young-Farmers.aspx

GROW WISCONSIN DAIRY

The organization's Dairy 30x20 grants have an intention of helping farmers to plan for future projects, identify ways to increase profits or transfer their farm onto the next generation. Funds can be used to add a consultant to a farmer's team who can help facilitate operational changes that will benefit the farm's profitability and strengthen the WISCONSIN dairy industry. Grants amount up to $5,000 and are to be used to hire consultants with the expertise to address the individual needs of the specific farm in question. Cost share payments by the farmer are required at 20% of the total grant amount. January deadline. See website for application details.
See: www.datcp.wi.gov/Farms/Dairy_Farming/index.aspx

CARROLL J. HAAS FOUNDATION

The Carroll J. Haas Foundation provides funding for agriculture, animals, preservation and protection, among other causes, mainly in MICHIGAN. Grants are $50,000 or less. Submit a letter of inquiry by December 31st.
Write: Carroll J. Haas, 27020 Simpson Road, Mendon, MI 49072

THE HARDEN FOUNDATION

The Harden Foundation awards grants to non-profit organizations in Monterey County CALIFORNIA, with an emphasis on the Salinas Valley area. The Foundation has several areas of interest including Agricultural Education. General support, project support and one-time capital grant requests are considered annually with amounts ranging from $5,000 to $100,000. Deadlines are March 1st and September 1st..
See: www.hardenfoundation.org

THE HERB SOCIETY OF AMERICA

The Herb Society awards grants and scholarships for education regarding herbs within the UNITED STATES. Grant/scholarship amounts and deadlines vary depending on the program. See website for application details.
See: www.herbsociety.org

HOBART CENTER FOR FOODSERVICE SUSTAINABILITY

The Hobart Center promotes foodservice sustainability within the UNITED STATES to corporations and individuals operating in the food service and food retail industry. Grants of $5,000 are awarded to honor the individual or company submitting a sustainability case study judged as the most innovative and best-executed foodservice sustainability project of the year. February deadline.
See: www.sustainablefoodequipment.com/hobart-center-for-foodservice-sustainability/

THE HOME DEPOT GARDEN CLUB

The Club's Youth Garden Grants support schools and community organizations with child-centered garden programs. Applying programs must include at least 15 children between the ages of 3 and 18 years. Five programs will receive gift cards valued at $1,000 while ninety-five additional programs will receive a $500 gift card. Deadline of December 3rd.
See: www.gardenclub.homedepot.com/tag/youth-garden-grant/

HOOKED ON HYDROPONICS

Schools and organizations can apply to conduct a hydroponic project with youth. Check website for application details, program is currently being revamped.
See: www.pgta.org/

HORACE BACKUS YDLI SCHOLARSHIP FUND

The Fund is intended to support young dairy producers within the UNITED STATES who wish to attend the Holstein Foundation's Young Dairy Leaders Institute, a unique and exciting program for young dairy producers and industry professionals. See website for application details.
See:
www.holsteinfoundation.org/contribute/backus_scholarship.html

HOWARD COUNTY ECONOMIC DEVELOPMENT AUTHORITY

The Authority has many grant and financing programs available to start or diversify agricultural enterprise in MARYLAND. The Authority's Agricultural Innovation Grant hopes to encourage Howard County's agricultural crop or livestock producers or processors to expand or diversify their business operations, engage in research and development, production buildings, major fixtures, processing facilities or address other business needs. Matching funds and/or materials of an equal amount required. July 15 deadline; grant amounts range from $1,000 to $10,000.
See: www.hceda.org/farms-agriculture/start-a-new-farm/grants-and-financing.aspx

HYDRO HARVEST FARMS

The organization lists school gardening grants available for educators in the UNITED STATES on their website.
See:
www.hydroharvestfarms.com/grantsforschoolgardens.html

ILLINIOS DEPARTMENT OF AGRICULTURE

The Department has a variety of agricultural grant programs designed to benefit rural residents, communities and other groups in ILLINOIS. Programs include a Sustainable Agriculture grant as well as a grant program designed specifically for specialty crops. Grant deadlines and amounts vary by program. Application information can be found online.
See: www.agr.state.il.us/grants

INDIANA'S FAMILY OF FARMERS

The organization's goal is to offer grants for local communities to underscore the promotion of agriculture in INDIANA. Grants of up to $2,000 are made to improve educational agriculture-related events around Indiana. Funding is to be given to educational or outreach events focused on food and fiber. Applicants can also request money to make capital investments or safety upgrades. There is an emphasis on projects carried out by youth organizations such as FFA, with youth leadership in mind. Deadline is May 31st.
See: www.indianafamilyoffarmers.com

INSTITUTE FOR RURAL AMERICA

The Institute's Seize the Moment Grants are designed to assist non-profit organizations within the UNITED STATES needing to take quick action on issues that arise, but have not been budgeted for, in addition to organizations who wish to send staff to local, regional or national training programs in their field. Maximum grant amount of $250. no deadlines. See website for application details.
See:
www.instituteruralamerica.org/html/seize_the_moment_gr ants.html
See: www.ruralusa.org/html/grants.html

IOBY

This organization intends crowd-funding in order to support citizen-led, neighbor-funded projects. Their goal is to connect people to environmental projects in their own neighborhoods. No deadlines.
See: www.ioby.org/idea

IOWA DEPARTMENT OF AGRICULTURE

The organization's Soil and Water Conservation District offices can be contacted by local farmers to apply for up to 50% of costs for projects to install conservation practices throughout IOWA. The organization hopes to increase conservation practices which prevent erosion and better protect water quality in the state. See website for application details.
See:
www.iowaagriculture.gov/press/2014press/press08042014.asp

KANSAS COMMUNITY GARDENS

With funds by the Kansas Health Foundation and operated by K-State Research and Extension, the project offers grants to communities to request up to $5,000 to start a new garden. A complementary effort called Get Growing Kansas City offers mini grants up to $3,000 to urban farmers and community gardens toward new and expanded farms and community gardens to produce and improve access to fresh food for low income residents of Kansas City, MISSOURI, Jackson county, MISSOURI and Wyandotte and Johnson counties in KANSAS.
See: www.getgrowingkc.org and www.kansascommunitygardens.org

KANSAS RURAL CENTER
The Center partners with organizations, agencies, companies and individuals to provide the resources that farmers, ranchers, consumers and communities need to grow an ecological, diversified food and farming system. They provide many program areas for farmers in the state of KANSAS, as well as across the UNITED STATES to gather research, information and funding for their agricultural projects. Currently, funding and supplies are available for those looking to install polytunnels in order to extend their growing season, as well as those interested in adding beekeeping to their repertoire of farming skills. Programs shift often, check website for current offerings. See website for application details.
See: www.kansasruralcenter.org/our-projects/

KATIE'S KROPS
The organization's grant program offers funding to youth between the ages of 9 and 16 in the UNITED STATES to start vegetable gardens with the harvest then being donated to feed people in need in their area. Grants of up to $400 in the form of a gift card to the garden center of their choice are awarded in addition to a digital camera to document the garden and harvest. Deadline of December 31st. See website for application details.
See: www.katieskrops.com/apply-for-a-grant.html

KEEP AMERICA BEAUTIFUL
The organization strives to bring people together to build and sustain vibrant communities. They provide several grant programs annually, with varying award amounts and deadlines. See website for current grant programs and application information.
See: www.kab.org

W.K. KELLOGG FOUNDATION
The Foundation seeks to work with communities to create conditions for vulnerable children so that they can realize their full potential in school, work and life. Grants go to programs and projects which seek to improve the health of children, among other areas of interest. Non-profits can apply to establish new activities that transform food deserts into food oasis's improving the food system to deliver healthier food to all children. Online application. Grant making is prioritized in MICHIGAN, MISSISSIPPI, NEW MEXICO, NEW ORLEANS, HAITI and MEXICO. Grant amounts and deadlines vary. See website for application details.
See: www.wkkf.org/grantseekers

KENTUCKY AGRICULTURAL DEVELOPMENT FUND
The Fund's County Agricultural Investment Program (CAIP) is designed to provide farmers within KENTUCKY with incentives to allow them to improve and diversify their current production practices. Funding is provided for innovative proposals that increase net farm income and affect tobacco farmers, tobacco-impacted communities and agriculture across the state by stimulating markets for Kentucky agricultural products, finding new ways to add value to Kentucky agricultural products, and exploring new opportunities for Kentucky farms. Funding is provided through a 1:1 cost-share agreement between the farmer and the CAIP. Maximum grant is $2,500 with applications are by January 9th. See website for application details.
See: www.agpolicy.ky.gov/funds/Pages/default.aspx

KENTUCKY STATE UNIVERSITY

The University's Small Scale Farm Grant Program is administered through the University's College of Agriculture, Food Science, and Sustainable Systems' Center for Sustainability of Farms and Families. The College's mission is to provide assistance and development in aquaculture farming & marketing, certified organic farming & marketing and value-added enterprise development. The Small Scale Farm Grant Program was developed to support expansion of certain types of agriculture in Kentucky, especially among certain underserved groups. Grant funding decisions are based upon the impact the grant is expected to have on the production and sales of KENTUCKY grown or raised farm products. Grants amount $5,000 for individuals and no more than $15,000 for organizations that benefit multiple farms. June deadline. See website for application details.

See: www.kysu.edu/academics/cafsss/cafsss-research-areas/cafsss-small-scale-farm-grant-program/

KEURIG GREEN MOUNTAIN

The company's Employee Community Grant Program helps address specific issues aligned with their business values and community needs within the UNITED STATES and CANADA, with a particular area of interest being strengthening local food systems. See website for application details.

See: www.keuriggreenmountain.com

THE KERR CENTER FOR SUSTAINABLE AGRICULTURE

The Kerr Center for Sustainable Agriculture offers a free Beginning Farmer and Rancher Program for farmers in OKLAHOMA and surrounding states with experience less than 10 years or have a gross farm income of less than $150,000. The course consists of five Saturday training workshops. Participants choose to follow either a livestock or horticulture track. The program will provide beginning farmers and ranchers with the information and techniques they need to be successful. Application deadline of November 15th. See website for application details.
See: www.kerrcenter.com

KRESGE FOUNDATION

The Kresge Foundation promotes the physical health and well-being of low-income and vulnerable populations by impacting environmental and social conditions affecting them. One focus area is Emerging and Promising Practices in Population Health which includes multi-sector strategies that address policy, environmental and programmatic changes with a special focus on food systems. Non-profit organizations and government entities within the UNITED STATES may apply. No deadlines. See website for application details.
See: http://www.kresge.org/programs/health

LAKEWINDS ORGANIC FIELD FUND
The Fund's goal is to support local farmers and farming associations with preference in MINNESOTA, northern IOWA and western WISCONSIN. Grant applicants should be working on the development and sustainability of organics through research and development, organic certification, transitioning farms to organic means, creating new farms and land trust creation for organic farms. Grants amount less than $8,000. February deadline. See website for application details.
See: www.lakewinds.com/community/loff/

LAND O' LAKES FOUNDATION
The Land O' Lakes Foundation offers a variety of community grants and scholarships to rural communities. The John Brandt Memorial Scholarship program is a $25,000 scholarship available to graduate students pursuing dairy related-degrees at Iowa State University, South Dakota State University, The University of Minnesota, Twin Cities, or the University of Wisconsin, Madison. Additional grants awarded include Community Grants, which provide funding for projects focused on hunger, education and community giving. Grant amounts and deadlines vary, see website for program and application details.
See: www.landolakesinc.com/company/corporateresponsibility/foundation/johnbrandt/ or
www.foundation.landolakes.com/

FRITZ LANG FOUNDATION

The Foundation awards scholarships for agri-science education, among other areas. The Foundation's goal is to improve the quality of life for LOUISIANA's Vermilion and Jefferson Davis Parish farm families through extending educational opportunities for local graduating high school students and current college students studying within the Agriculture field. Grants are for $1,200 per semester. Deadline of April 1st.
See: www.fritzlangfoundation.org/scholarships.html

LAWN & LANDSCAPE and GIE MEDIA

Lawn & Landscape, and its parent company, GIE Media, has established an annual fund of two $2,500 academic scholarships for outstanding college students working toward a degree in horticulture, environmental science or other field related to a segment of the green industry. Applicants must be enrolled in a recognized two or four year college or university. Deadline of April 15th. See website for application details.
See: www.lawnandlandscape.com/horticultural-scholarship.aspx

LEOPOLD CENTER FOR SUSTAINABLE AGRICULTURE

The Center supports projects in a variety of areas that enhance sustainability for IOWA agriculture. Grants given fund research, education and demonstration projects in Ecology, Marketing and Food Systems, Policy and Cross-Cutting. Iowa non-profit and educational organizations may apply. Deadline of July 8th.
See: http://www.leopold.iastate.edu/grants/current
Also find their compilation of funding sources at
www.leopold.iastate.edu/pubs-and-papers/2014-10-funding-opportunities-local-foods

THE CHARLES A AND ANNE MORROW LINDBERGH FOUNDATION

The Lindbergh foundation funds grants that improve the quality of life offering balance between nature and technology. Grants of up to $10,580 are awarded annually in numerous areas of interest, including agriculture. See website for application details.

See: www.lindberghfoundation.org/docs/index.php/about-us/programs

LOCAL FOOD FUND

Support to innovative projects that result in improved access to, demand for, and awareness of local food in ONTARIO. For-profit, non-profit, and public organizations may apply for grants of up to $50,000. No deadlines.

See: www.omafra.gov.on.ca/english/about/local_food_fund.htm

LORRIE OTTO

Established by Wild Ones, the Lorrie Otto Seeds for Education Grant Program gives small grants to schools, nature centers, and other non-profits to enhance and develop an appreciation for nature using native plants. Projects such as wildflower gardens as habitat, rainwater gardens, and native plants in an outdoor classroom must emphasize students and volunteers involvement in all phases of development and increase the educational value of the site. Cash awards range from $100 to $500 for the purchase of native plants and seed. Application deadline of October 15th.

See: www.wildones.org/seeds-for-education

THE LUMPKIN FAMILY FOUNDATION

The Lumpkin Family Foundation supports innovation and long-lasting improvements in the environment, health, education, and community access to the arts. They offer grants to non-profit organizations and municipalities which improve the overall wellness of people's lives and have a special interest in healthy food production and production, especially in east central ILLINOIS. Applications due by April 14th. See website for application details.
See: www.lumpkinfoundation.org/HOWtoapply/GrantSeekers.aspx

MAINE DEPARTMENT OF AGRICULTURE, CONSERVATION AND FORESTRY

The Department's Agricultural Development Grant Program is intended to provide cost-share funding to agricultural producers and food processors for innovative projects in market promotion, market research and development, value-added processing and new technology demonstration in MAINE. Grant amounts and deadlines vary. See website for application details.
See: www.maine.gov

MAINE FARMLAND TRUST

The Trust makes grants of up $3,000 to projects or programs submitted by nonprofit organizations, schools, community groups, or individuals that increase food sustainability and improve the health and well-being of Blue Hill Peninsula residents and aim to create a more just and sustainable local food system through food production, education, or related projects. The 2015 deadline was in February with grant awards made by the end of March. Contact strunzo@mainefarmlandtrust.org or call 338-6575 with questions.
See: mainefarmlandtrust.org

MASSACHUSETTS DEPARTMENT OF AGRICULTURE
The organization's Matching Enterprise Grants for
Agriculture was created to help with business improvements
on new farms within MASSACHUSETTS. The program
provides selected participants with business planning and
technical assistance, followed by funds for farm
improvement strategies. Grants are made on a 1:1 cash-
matching basis with a maximum of $10,000 provided. The
program's objective is to assist beginning farmers who aspire
to develop their farms into commercially viable operations
in their first through fifth year of business. Deadline in June.
See website for application details.
See: www.mass.gov

**MASSACHUSETTS SOCIETY FOR PROMOTING
AGRICULTURE**
The Society focuses funding on sustainable agriculture
projects, projects which directly benefit the farming
community and projects which carry ancillary benefits, all
for the agricultural community of MASSACHUSETTS.
Grants typically amount around $5,000. No deadlines. See:
www.promotingmassag.org

MANTIS
The company provides Mantis Awards every year to
charitable and educational garden projects that enhance the
quality of life in host communities. Past applicants have
received Mantis tillers/cultivators. Any non-profit garden
within the UNITED STATES may apply. March deadline.
See: www.kidsgardening.com

THE J.W. MCCONNELL FAMILY FOUNDATION

The only provides support to registered Canadian charities for projects taking place in CANADA and does not provide support to local projects, except as part of a national initiative. Sustainability is one of its primary initiatives. The foundation envisions a food system that links growers and consumers in supply chains that incorporate shared values around sustainability, health, and resilience. Check the website for new posted Requests for Proposals (RFP's). There is also an online eligibility and application system for screening and accepting unsolicited proposals.
See: www.mcconnellfoundation.ca/en/granting

GEORGINE B. MCDONALD TRUST

The Trust awards scholarships to students from Douglas County, ILLINOIS pursuing a career In agriculture, as well as other careers.
Write: Georgine B McDonald Trust Scholarship, c/o Tuscola National Bank, 900 S. Progress Blvd Tuscola, IL 61953

THE MCLEAN FOUNDATION

Among the McLean Foundation's areas of interest is Conservation, which, in the past, has included farm-related projects. Grants made by the Foundation are restricted to non-profit organizations in CANADA. Applications are reviewed on an ongoing basis. See website for application details.
See: www.mcleanfoundation.ca/applications.html

MELINDA GRAY ARDIA ENVIRONMENTAL FOUNDATION

The Foundation's grant program seeks to contribute to the development, implementation and/or field testing of environmental curricula which integrates field activities and classroom teaching as well as incorporates basic ecological principles and problem solving. Organizations such as schools, non-profits, government agencies and others across the globe are eligible to apply. Grants amount up to $1,500. Pre-proposals are due by September 14th. See website for application details.
See: www.mgaef.org

MERCK FAMILY FUND

The Merck Family Fund supports non-profit organizations in cities within NEW ENGLAND, NEW YORK, NEW JERSEY and Philadelphia, PENNSYLVANIA that are harnessing the power of young people to create urban farms and local markets in food insecure communities. The Fund promotes local production and distribution of fresh, healthy and affordable food. Funding decisions are made in May and November, with Letters of Inquiry reviewed on a rolling basis throughout the year. See website for application details.
See: www.merckff.org

JOHN MERCK FUND

The Fund supports Regional Food Systems, in addition to other areas of interest. Grants awarded are designed to strengthen innovation and entrepreneurship of non-profit organizations in NEW ENGLAND by funding initiatives to develop institutional demand and the regional supply network. Interested organizations may send a brief letter or email of inquiry. Deadline of December 31st. See website for details.
See: www.jmfund.org/grant.php

MICHIGAN ALLIANCE FOR ANIMAL AGRICULTURE

The Alliance was designed to enhance the advancement of the animal agriculture economy in MICHIGAN. Their grant program seeks projects which suit their goals, address critical needs relevant to Michigan's Animal Agriculture Industries and are requested within the categories of Applied Research (maximum budget of $50,000), Extension (maximum budget of $30,000) and Seed Grants (maximum budget of $25,000). Principal Investigators must be employed by Michigan State University. Proposals due by September 1st. Application details can be found online. See:
www.agbioresearch.msu.edu/uploads/396/36186/RFP_201 5_M-AAA.pdf

MICHIGAN DEPARTMENT OF AGRICULTURE & RURAL DEVELOPMENT

The state agency has many grant, loan and funding opportunities available for those working within the areas of farm, business and lab services within the state of MICHIGAN. Examples of recent award areas include proposals intended to establish, retain, expand, attract and/or develop value added agricultural processing and/or developing regional food systems as well as proposals wishing to enhance the competitiveness of specialty crops by way of research, promotion, marketing,trade enhancement and food safety, among other methods. Grant amounts and grant deadlines vary by program, check website for application details.
See: www.michigan.gov/mdard

MICHIGAN ENERGY OFFICE

The Office is offering matching grants for energy efficiency retrofit projects in commercial buildings that are owned by small businesses and private non-profit organizations with fewer than 100 employees in MICHIGAN. These grants are designed to encourage cost-effective energy upgrades that reduce operating costs for building owners, support local job creation and free up capital to re-invest in these businesses over the long term. Grants range in amount from $5,000 to $20,000. Applicants must provide a minimum cash match equal to 100% of their grant fund request. Applications are due by August 31st. See link for application details.
See: www.michiganbusiness.org/cm/Files/Public-Notices-Requests-for-Proposals/2014_Energy_Efficiency_Bldg_Retrofits_RFP/EE-Bldg-Retrofits-RFP.pdf

MICHIGAN VEGETABLE COUNCIL

The Council's primary mission is to advance vegetable production in MICHIGAN. Funding is awarded to research and educational programs, as well as educational scholarships. Grants are made by way of a recommendation from the Council's Board of Directors. Proposal areas change annually. Scholarships are awarded to undergraduate and graduate students at Michigan State University, as well as other midwestern universities, with a target amount of $1,000 given. See website for application details.
See: www.michiganvegetablecouncil.org

MIDWEST DAIRY ASSOCIATION
The Association offers scholarships within the UNITED STATES to students who are either from dairy farms or are studying within a dairy-related major. Eligibility and awards vary by state with available scholarships shifting throughout the year. Deadline of March 1st. See website for application details. See:
www.midwestdairycheckoff.com/0t23p41/scholarships/

MINNESOTA DEPARTMENT OF AGRICULTURE
The Department's Sustainable Agriculture Demonstration Grant Program is designed for individuals or groups for on-farm sustainable agriculture research or demonstration projects in MINNESOTA. Grants of up to $25,000 are awarded to fund practices that promote environmental stewardship and conservation of resources as well as improve profitability and quality of life on farms and in rural areas. Minnesota farmers, educational institutions, students, and non-profit organizations may apply. The Department's Livestock Investment Grant Program is designed to allow eligible livestock producers to support their industry and stay competitive. Qualifying producers are to be reimbursed ten percent of the first $500,000 of investment, with a minimum investment of $4,000. Qualifying expenditures include the purchase, construction, or improvement of buildings or facilities for the production of livestock, and the purchase of fencing as well as feeding and waste management equipment. Producers who suffered a loss due to a natural disaster or unintended consequence may also apply. The grant will not pay for livestock or land purchases or for the cost of debt refinancing. Maximum grant amount per year is $25,000 with an application deadline of December 10th. The Department's Farm to School Grant Program was created in order to increase sales of agricultural products to elementary schools, secondary

schools and child care centers. Grants are awarded to stimulate purchases of locally grown and raised food products. Public or private schools or school districts that are a part of the National School Lunch Program and serve food to preschool and/or K-12 students may apply. Grants range in amount from $1,000 to $30,000. Proposal deadline of November 3rd. See website for application details.
See: www.mda.state.mn.us/grants/

MINNESOTA AGRICULTURE IN THE CLASSROOM
Minnesota Agriculture in the Classroom (MAITC) offers Ag Literacy Grants for up to $400 to K-12 teachers wishing to bring agriculture to life in the classroom, school garden or a field trip to agriculture processing sites. The goal is to provide a financial incentive for teachers to effectively integrate agricultural content into core academic subjects like science, social studies or language arts. The deadline was Jan. 10 in 2015. Online grant application.
See: www.mda.state.mn.us/maitc

MONTANA DEPARTMENT OF AGRICULTURE
The Department supports the development of agricultural pursuits in MONTANA. The Department has many areas of grant and loan opportunities, including opportunities for young farmers, rural community development and FFA organizations. Grant amounts and deadlines vary by program area. See website for application details.
See:
www.agr.mt.gov/agr/Programs/Development/GrantsLoans/
The Department's "Growth Through Agriculture" grants and loans are intended to add value to Montana's agricultural products as well as to create jobs in MONTANA. Recent application deadlines in September and January. See:
www.agr.mt.gov/agr/Programs/Development/GrantsLoans/GTA/

THE RALPH K. MORRIS FOUNDATION

The Foundation's Cooperative Leadership Fund provides financial support to help cover costs associated with training, professional development and educational programs for rural young leaders interested in the future of cooperatives and rural communities. Grants range in amount from $300 to $500 and applicants must be sponsored by an organization. No deadlines. See website for application details.
See: www.ralphkmorrisfoundation.org

THE MOSAIC COMPANY FOUNDATION

The Foundation provides grants for USA and international non-profit organizations that are working to help people grow the food and they need develop communities in FLORIDA, ILLINOIS, KENTUCKY, LOUISIANA, MICHIGAN, NEW MEXICO and TEXAS, as well as INDIA, CHINA, ARGENTINA, CHILE and BRAZIL. Funds support innovative programs or projects focusing on food, water and local community development. Rolling deadlines. See website for further details.
See:
www.mosaicco.com/sustainability/or_how_to_apply.htm

NALITH, INC

Nalith, Inc. provides support for the promotion of research and development of natural organic farming methods and promotion of vegetarianism and vegetarian lifestyles to enhance good health. Non-profit organizations within the UNITED STATES may apply. No deadlines. Grants amount $25,000 or less.
Write: 13611 S. Dixie Highway 109-514, Miami, FL 33176

NATIONAL CHILDREN'S CENTER FOR RURAL AND AGRICULTURAL HEALTH + SAFETY

The organization's mini-grant program is designed to support small-scale projects and pilot studies that address prevention of childhood agricultural disease and injury. Funds are allocated to support projects that test innovative strategies, develop new partnerships beyond safety professionals, and/or translate research findings into practical applications. Individuals affiliated with community-based organizations, public or private institutions, units of local or state government, or tribal government throughout the UNITED STATES are eligible to apply. Grants of up to $20,000 will be awarded with a deadline of December 1st. See website for application details. See: www3.marshfieldclinic.org/nccrahs/default.aspx?page=ncc rahs_minigrants

NATIONAL CORN GROWERS ASSOCIATION

The National Corn Growers Association awards scholarships to undergraduate and graduate students studying in an agriculture-related field who are members of the NCGA or whose parents are members. Scholarships amount $1,000. College sophomores and above may apply. Applications must be submitted by December. See website for application details.
See: www.ncga.com/topics/college-scholarships

NATIONAL FARMERS

National Farmers (NFO, Inc.) offers $1,000 Farm Kids for College scholarships to High School seniors within the UNITED STATES who plan to pursue an agriculture degree at a college or university. March deadline. See website for application details.
See: www.nfo.org/Scholarships/default.aspx

NATIONAL FFA ORGANIZATION

The Organization's Supervised Agricultural Experiences (SAE) grants are designed for current FFA members in the UNITED STATES grade 7-11 with a demonstrated financial need who wish to initiate or improve their SAE. Deadline of November 15th. See website for application details.
See:
www.ffa.org/programs/grantsandscholarships/SAEGrants/Pages/default.aspx

NATIONAL GARDEN CLUB

The National Garden Club is offering cash awards to clubs, groups of clubs and states for projects that include some native plants and/or wildflowers. Awards of up to $1,000 are available. Additionally, the Club offers grants of up to $500 to be used towards direct expenses for an educational program involving native plants and/or wildflowers. State Garden Clubs, districts, councils and individual garden clubs may co-sponsor a symposium with state agencies, arboreta, native plant societies, or similar organizations. See website for application details.
See: www.gardenclub.org/awards/wildflower-awardgrants.aspx

NATIONAL GARDENING ASSOCIATION

The Association's Youth Garden Grant is open to any school or organization within the UNITED STATES planning to grow a garden with at least 15 children between the ages of 3 and 18. Grant packages include a $500 gift certificate to the Gardening with Kids online store, curriculum, seeds, a pair of gardening gloves, a window garden box, plant starts and a tool package, along with a raised garden bed. Applications are due by December 5th. Check website for additional grants and funding opportunities for youth and educators.
See: www.kidsgardening.org

NATIONAL INSTITUTE OF FOOD AND AGRICULTURE

The Institute's Community Food Projects grant program is designed to fund three types of grants: Community Food Projects, Planning Projects and Training and Technical Assistance Projects. Public food program service providers, tribal organizations, or private non-profit entities, including gleaners, within the UNITED STATES may apply. Grants of up to $250,000 are available, with matching funds required for most projects. Application deadline of March 31st. See website for application details.
See:
www.nifa.usda.gov/funding/rfas/community_food.html

NATIONAL JERSEY YOUTH SCHOLARSHIPS

The scholarship program supports educational opportunities for Jersey youth within the UNITED STATES enrolled in post-secondary institutions and on-farm internships. A variety of scholarships are awarded each year. Deadline of July 1st. See website for application details.
See:
www.usjersey.com/YouthProgram/scholarshipinfo.html

NATIONAL MEAT ASSOCIATION FOUNDATION (NMA)

NMA Scholarships are awarded to encourage undergraduate students to pursue a degree in animal, meat or food sciences. Scholarships amount around $2,500 with an application deadline of May 30th. See website for application details.
See: www.meatscholars.org

NATIONAL RESTAURANT ASSOCIATION EDUCATIONAL FOUNDATION

The NRAEF Scholarship Program provides funding for the restaurant and food service industry and sponsors awards for educators, undergraduates and high school seniors as well. These individuals must have an interest in food service/hospitality. Scholarship amounts and deadlines vary by program. See website for application details.
See: www.nraef.org/scholarships/

NATIONAL SHEEP INDUSTRY IMPROVEMENT CENTER

The national sheep Industry Improvement center offers and accepts grant proposals. The center has approximately $1 million dollars available in grant funds. The Center's Sheep Production and Marketing Grant Program creates new opportunities for growth and innovation within the sheep industry. Funding is intended for projects which strengthen and enhance the production and marketing of sheep products in the UNITED STATES through infrastructure improvement, business and resource development and the development of innovative approaches to solving long-term needs. Grants of up to $300,000 will be available with a deadline of November 22nd. See website for application details.
See: www.nsiic.org

NATIONAL SUSTAINABLE AGRICULTURE INFORMATION SERVICE

The Service lists Sustainable Farming Internships and Apprenticeships on its website as a tool to help farmers and apprentices connect with each other. It is available for farms in the UNITED STATES and its territories, with a few listings in CANADA and the CARIBBEAN.
See: www.attra.ncat.org/attra-pub/internships/

NATURE SACRED
The Program National Nature Sacred Awards Programs seeks to fund the best example of new sacred public green space which combines a high quality design-build with rigorous research about user impacts. Six projects are funded each year. See website for application details.
See: www.naturesacred.org/national-awards/overview/

NATURE'S PATH ORGANIC FOODS
Nature's Path Organic Foods, in partnership with Organic Gardening Magazine, has continued its active support of urban agriculture with their Gardens for Good grant contest. The contest empowers non-profit organizations to take action and grow organically. Three non-profits within the UNITED STAES and CANADA are awarded $15,000 toward organic community garden projects. Winning communities may receive a combination of cash, technical assistance, products and more. June deadline. See website for application details.
See: www.us.naturespath.com/about/movements/gardens-for-good

NEW BELGIUM BREWING COMPANY
The organization's Environmental Stewardship Grants Program is intended to serve and connect with the communities in which they sell their products. They support Sustainable Agriculture projects, among other areas of interest. Projects centered on soil, water, healthy work environments, collaborative relationships and urban farming are most applicable. Geographic restrictions change annually, check website for details. Grants of up to $10,000 are awarded. Applications are accepted through May 31st. See website for application details.
See:
www.newbelgium.com/sustainability/Community/Philanthropy.aspx

NEW ENGLAND GRASSROOTS ENVIRONMENT FUND

The Fund seeks to energize and nurture long term civic engagement in local initiatives that create and maintain healthy, just, safe and environmentally sustainable communities within CONNECTICUT, MAINE, MASSACHUSETTS, NEW HAMPSHIRE, RHODE ISLAND and VERMONT. The Fund provides grants for groups/projects that are just beginning (Seed Grants) with amounts ranging from $250-$1,000 as well as for those that are already underway (Grow Grants) with amounts ranging from $1,000 to $3,500. Issuing areas include Food, among other pursuits. No deadlines. See website for application details.
See: www.grassrootsfund.org

NEWMAN'S OWN FOUNDATION

Newman's Own Foundation has committed more than $10 million in grants over three years to support initiatives that increase fresh food access and nutrition education in underserved communities. Grants will be awarded to 36 non-profit organizations around the country that provide programs and services to improve nutrition. The Foundation is also forming a Nutrition Cohort of six non-profits and a research university each with distinctive expertise and programming, to collaborate and collectively pursue greater impact with the goal of helping to improve health among children and families in underserved communities through fresh food access and nutrition education.
See: www.newmansownfoundation.org

NEW MEXICO FARMERS' MARKETING ASSOCIATION (NMFMA)

The NMFMA, in cooperation with the Permaculture Guild and Permaculture Credit Union initiative, developed a low interest micro-loan program for small scale farmers who sell at NEW MEXICO farmer's markets. Loans are from $500 to $3,000 and must be paid back within 40 months. Check current guidelines and rates on websites.
See: www.farmersmarketsnm.org or www.permacultureguild.org

NORTH CAROLINA COOPERATIVE EXTENSION

The organization provides grants to family farms through support from the NC Tobacco Trust Fund Commission. Grants range in size from $5,000 to $10,000 but will allow applications up to $15,000 if strong justification is demonstrated. Eligible grant applicants are those who are agriculturally dependent, earning at least 50% of their personal income from their farm operation. Grants are intended for projects which present a new direction or opportunity to diversify, expand or implement new entrepreneurial plans for their farm operations.
Former/current tobacco growers or former quota holders receive higher priority. Applications due in December. See website for application details.
See: www.ces.ncsu.edu

NORTH CAROLINA TOBACCO TRUST FUND COMMISSION

The Commission seeks to mitigate the general decline in the tobacco-related segment of NORTH CAROLINA's economy. Funding is available to the public for alleviating or avoiding unemployment and quantifiable adverse fiscal impacts, stabilizing local tobacco-dependent communities and tax bases and to provide for the optimal use of natural resources. Government organizations, non-profit organizations and members of the private sector may apply by March 5th. See website for application details.
See: www.tobaccotrustfund.org

NORTH CENTRAL REGION-SARE

The organization's mission is to advance innovations in American agriculture that improve profitability, stewardship and quality of life by investing in groundbreaking research and education. There are four different areas funded by the organization, which are available in ILLINOIS, INDIANA, IOWA, KANSAS, MICHIGAN, MINNESOTA, MISSOURI, NEBRASKA, NORTH DAKOTA, OHIO, SOUTH DAKOTA and WISCONSIN. There are Research and Education Grants, Farmer Rancher Grants, Graduate Student Grants and Youth Educator Grants and/or Professional Development Grants available for those who qualify. Grant deadlines and amounts vary by program. See website for application details.
See: www.northcentralsare.org

NORTHEAST ORGANIC FARMING ASSOC. OF VERMONT (NOFA)
The NOFA Vermont Farmer Emergency Fund is available to assist VERMONT certified organic and NOFA Vermont member commercial farmers who have been adversely affected by natural and unnatural disasters such as crop failure, field flooding, fire, barn collapse, etc. Assistance includes a 12 month zero percent interest loan of up to $2,500 with additional funds as available. Repayment by the recipient takes place on a flexible schedule - or the loan may be repaid by donations to the fund. Farmers may request grants up to $2,500. Farmers may also be eligible to request loans from NOFA's Farmer Loan Fund with a current interest rate of 5.75%. See website for application details. A listing of other financial resources, including grants, is available on the NOFA website.
See: www.nofavt.org/programs/farm-financial-resources/farmer-emergency-fund

NORTHWEST FARM CREDIT SERVICES
The organization is committed to improving the economic and social well-being of rural communities in ALASKA, IDAHO, MONTANA, OREGON and WASHINGTON. Their Rural Community Grant Program provides money for projects such as building or improving facilities; purchasing necessary equipment to facilitate a program; and funding capital improvements which improve a community's infrastructure, viability and/or prosperity. Grants range in amount from $500 to $5,000. February and October deadlines.
See: www.northwestfcs.com

NO SMALL POTATOES INVESTMENT CLUB
The Club's mission is to strengthen the local food economy in MAINE by awarding small loans to farms, fishermen, and the food businesses they supply to help them thrive. They give low-interest loans of $5,000 or less at a 5% annual interest rate for terms of up to three years without collateral. There are multiple rounds of loan-giving each year. See website for application details.
See: www.nosmallpotatoesinvestmentclub.com/

JESSIE SMITH NOYES FOUNDATION
The Foundation makes grants nationwide to non-profit organizations which promote healthy, just and sustainable agriculture and natural environment programs. Grants range in amount from $10,000 to $30,000 with applications accepted year-round. See website for application details.
See: www.noyes.org

OHIO FARM BUREAU FOUNDATION

The Foundation awards scholarships to encourage students from all walks of life to pursue opportunities in agriculture within OHIO. Applications are due in March for the Cindy Hollingshead Scholarship Fund, the Darwin Bryan Scholarship Fund, the Women's Leadership in Agriculture Scholarship Program, and the Ohio Farm Bureau Foundation Scholar (OFBFS) award. The website also includes scholarships offered by county farm bureaus. The Foundation also offers Agriculture Action & Awareness Grants to community service groups in rural, suburban and/or urban settings, independent producers and/or agricultural producer groups wishing to initiate, continue and/or complete a program that highlighted agriculture and its impact on community economics, community development and/or agribusiness development. Grants range in amount between $1,000 and $3,000. Matching funds and/or resources are required. Deadline in November. See website for application details.
See: www.ofbf.org/foundation/scholarships-and-grants/

OKLAHOMA AGRICULTURE, FOOD & FORESTRY

The Department's Agriculture Enhancement and Diversification Program provides funds in the form of 0% interest loans or grants for the purpose of expanding the state's value added processing sector and to encourage farm diversification. Funds, provided on a cost-share basis, must be used for marketing and utilization, cooperative marketing, farm diversification and basic and applied research. Also supports those pursuing specialty crops. All proposals must demonstrate the ability to directly benefit OKLAHOMA farmers and ranchers. Applications are accepted year-round, however, proposals should be submitted at least 6 months prior to their anticipated start time. Grants amount up to $10,000. See:
www.ag.ok.gov/mktdev/aedp.htm

OLD ORCHARD BRANDS, LLC

Old Orchard Brand makes donations to a variety of local and regional nonprofit organizations that further its mission of encouraging healthy and active families. Applications accepted year-round for product donations or sponsorships. See website for application details.
See: www.oldorchard.com/about/contact/donation-requests

OMAHA WORLD HERALD FOUNDATION TRUST

The foundation makes awards primarily in the western Omaha NEBRASKA area and gives to a number of causes including agriculture.
Write: c/o Wells Fargo Bank NA, 1248 O Street 4th Floor, MAC N8032-042, Lincoln NE 68508

THE ONTARIO MINISTRY OF AGRICULTURE, FOOD AND RURAL AFFAIRS

The Department's multiple grant programs are designed to assist those within the farming, food or agricultural industries in ONTARIO. Cost-sharing funding opportunities of varying sizes and with varying deadlines can be accessed via the Department's website.
See: www.omafra.gov.on.ca/

ONTARIO TRILLIUM FOUNDATION

The Foundation supports non-profit organizations in CANANDA in a variety of different capacities with a variety of different grant opportunities; a healthy and sustainable environment being one of six focus areas. Grants are available for projects at the conceptual stage all the way through to projects that need help to reach their greater potential. Grant amounts and deadlines vary by program area. See website for application details.
See: www.otf.ca

OPAL APPLES

Opal Apples seeks to build holistic, sustainable communities by empowering members to put their dreams into action and then serve those most in need. The company's "Youth Make a Difference Initiative" awards funding to youth-based initiatives serving communities in the UNITED STATES where youth take leadership roles in the project. Food, agriculture and/or nutrition must be issues addressed within each applicant's project. Maximum grant amount of $20,000 with a deadline of February 28th. See website for application details.
See: www.opalapples.com/cause.aspx

ORGANIC CROP IMPROVEMENT ASSOCIATION INTERNATIONAL

The OCIA offers micro grants from $300 to $1,500 for organic research, organic education and other ideas, which support organic agriculture. Projects must benefit multiple producers, processors and/or consumers. Limitations may exist for the number of grants given within a single region. Deadlines for applications are in March and November.
See: www.ociaresearchandeducation.org/index.php/awards/micro-grants

ORANGE COUNTY ECONOMIC DEVELOPMENT GRANT

The Agriculture Economic Development grant program of Orange County NORTH CAROLINA is designed to assist local farmers in developing new sources of agricultural income. There is a small grant up to $1,000 and large grants of up to $10,000. Download the guidelines and application forms or call the Orange County Economic Development office at (919) 245-2325. Applications will be reviewed quarterly.
See: http://growinorangenc.com/news/business-investment-grant-program/

ORGANIC FARMING RESEARCH FOUNDATION

The Foundation's Grant Research Database shares insights into organic farming systems with all farmers who use or want to adopt organic practices. OFRF also offers funding opportunities of up to $15,000 to individual farmers, beginning farmers, ranchers, extension personnel, researchers and others from the U.S., CANADA and MEXICO to support educational activities and materials that are pertinent to organic agricultural production and/or marketing and are aimed at organic producers and/or those considering making the transition to organic certification. Deadlines for proposals are mid-May and mid-November. See: www.ofrf.org/research/database or www.ofrf.org/research/grants/grant-proposal-requirements

ORGANIC SEED ALLIANCE

The Alliance's Farmer Seed Stewardship initiative represents a network of farmers who identify themselves as "seed stewards." The initiative is intended to advance education, research and advocacy to support farmers' ability to save, breed, and produce seed. To join the network, applicants must be a farmer who produces, saves, or improves at least one seed variety on their farm for commercial production or on-farm use or who conducts on-farm research or variety trials. Additional funding resources can be found on the organization's website.
See: www.seedalliance.org/farmer_seed_stewardships

ORGANIC VALLEY

Organic Valley is a farmer owned organic dairy cooperative that gives donations to organizations that champion one of the following: family and independent farmers and rural community issues, organic research, education and promotion, parents, parents-to-be and child wellness, humane animal treatment, and, environmental education and preservation. The Farmers Advocating for Organics Farmer Committee accepts proposals from individuals and organizations who wish to fund projects or programs dedicated to furthering organic education, organic farming or product research, and organic advocacy. Grants under $5,000 are awarded on a rolling basis. Deadlines are February and September 1st each year.
See: www.organicvalley.coop/about-us/donations/

THE AMERICAN PASTURED POULTRY PRODUCERS ASSOC.

The Association is dedicated to encouraging the production, processing, and marketing of poultry raised on pasture. Each year a $500 scholarship is given to one individual, farm or organization in the UNITED STATES that can demonstrate an educational need directly related to pastured poultry. Deadline of October 31st.
See: www.apppa.org/

PIONEER HI-BRED

Pioneer Hi-Bred's Community Investment department provides charitable support in communities where Pioneer employees and their customers live and work. Non-profits, local schools and public charities with quality of life initiatives may apply; the focus is on food security, community betterment and science education. Grants amount up to $5,000. See website for application details.
See: www.pioneer.com or www.pioneer.com/home/site/about/business/pioneer-giving/

THE POLLINATION PROJECT

The Project seeks game-changing visionaries who are at the precipice of launching a new social change effort and need seed capital to get started in the area of community health and wellness, in addition to other funding areas. Grants of $1,000 are awarded to social entrepreneurs with a practical vision for doing good in the world. No deadlines. See website for application details.

See: www.thepollinationproject.org/apply-for-a-grant/

PRESBYTERIAN MISSION AGENCY

The Agency's mission is to work with congregations and partners around the globe to alleviate hunger and eliminate its causes. Their Presbyterian Hunger Program provides grants to non-profit organizations and Presbyterian congregations addressing hunger in the UNITED STATES. Grant areas include Development Assistance, Public Policy Advocacy, Lifestyle Integrity, Education and Interpretation and Direct Food Relief. Grants of up to $20,000 are available with a deadline of April 30th.

See:
www.presbyterianmission.org/ministries/hunger/what-we-do/

PRESBYTERIAN COMMITTEE ON THE SELF-DEVELOPMENT OF PEOPLE

The Presbyterian Committee on the Self-Development of People Presbyterian Church (U.S.A.) awards grants to groups with whom they partner. The project must benefit and be presented, owned and controlled by groups that are economically poor, oppressed, and disadvantaged. The proposed project must empower to make long-term changes that structures that perpetuate poverty, oppression and injustice. In the past, community garden efforts have been funded. No deadline. Download pre-application form.
See: www.gamc.pcusa.org/ministries/sdop/apply-grant/
See:
http://www.presbyterianmission.org/ministries/sdop/apply-grant/

THE PROFESSIONAL DAIRY PRODUCERS FOUNDATION

The Professional Dairy Producers Foundation (PDPF) awards grants to non-profit, educational programs within the UNITED STATES that meet the needs of dairy producers and communities and share the foundation's passion and vision for education in dairy communities. Grant dollars are available to those organizations with unique ideas in the following two focus areas: building producer professionalism, or maintaining public trust. Applications due in December and June. Organizations may apply for grants of up to $5,000. See website for application details.
See: www.dairyfoundation.org/grants.php

QUIVIRA COALITION

The Coalition's Clarence Burch Award is given to individuals and organizations who lead by example in promoting and accomplishing outstanding stewardship of private and/or public lands. Individuals, organizations, or projects directed by an organization within the conservation or ranching communities are eligible. The award amounts $20,000 with a deadline of September 1st.
See: www.quiviracoalition.org/Annual_Conference/Clarenc e_Burch_Awards/

RAUSCHENBERG FOUNDATION

The Foundation's grant program aspires to a vibrant, equitable and sustainable world through the power of creative problem solving. Grant-making attention is at present focused on the field of climate change, among other pursuits. The Climate Change Solutions Fund is intended to fund organizations in ways that both engage a broad public and recognize the catalytic roles culture and creativity can play in these endeavors. The Fund is inviting proposals from non-profit organizations as well as those sponsored by non-profits of all stripes so as to provide resources to either mitigate the causes of climate change or adapt to the new physical and social environments it generates, including low-emission agriculture while sustaining or improving food security. Applicants may request between $25,000 to $150,000 with up to 15% of overhead costs included. Deadline in December. See website for application details.
See: www.rauschenbergfoundation.org

THE REAL ESTATE FOUNDATION OF BRITISH COLUMBIA

The Foundation's mission is to support real estate and land use related to research, public and professional education, and law reform in order to transform land use attitudes and practices, thus contributing to resilient, healthy communities and natural environments. Non-profit organizations and Community Contribution Companies undertaking projects in BRITISH COLUMBIA are eligible to apply. The Foundation is not limited to supporting charitable organizations. Grants can support the projects of municipalities, regional districts, First Nations, senior government departments, professional associations and other societies. Priority for projects including access to fresh water, sustainable food systems and well-planned built environments. Rolling deadlines. See website for application details.
See: www.refbc.com

RED ANTS PANTS FOUNDATION

The Foundation supports women's leadership, working family farms and ranches, and rural communities in MONTANA. Organizations and individuals may apply for grants from $500 to $3,000. See website for application details.
See: www.redantspantsfoundation.org/

ROCKVILLE BANK FOUNDATION

The Foundation provides funding to non-profit organizations and scholarships to high school seniors pursuing agricultural studies within the range of Rockville Bank locations in CONNECTICUT. See website for application details.
See: www.bankatunited.com/About/Community-Commitment/Charitable-Giving/Rockville-Bank-Foundation

RODALE INSTITUTE

The Institute's "Your 2 Cents" fund works to unite producers, consumers, researchers and educators to launch the next generation of organic farmers. Funding priorities include scholarships for students of organic agriculture, support for new organic farmers, assistance for veterans who wish to establish new careers in organic farming and research projects on organic agriculture. Support is given to highly motivated individuals as well as well-managed non-profit organizations who address significant issues within the organic community. Grants range in size from $1,000 to $10,000 with deadlines of January 31st and September 30th. See website for application details
.See: www.rodaleinstitute.org/

RSF SOCIAL FINANCE

RSF Social Finance (RSF) is a pioneering non-profit financial services organization dedicated to transforming the way the world works with money by supporting breakthrough ideas at the intersection of social change and finance. One of its focus areas is Food and Agriculture, within which they encourage new economic models that support sustainable food and agriculture, while raising public awareness of the value of organic and Biodynamic farming.The RSF Seed Fund provides small grants of $500 to $5,000 to non-profit organizations within the UNITED STATES. March deadline. See website for application details.
See: www.rsfsocialfinance.org/services/giving/seedfund/apply-for-a-seed-fund-grant/

RURAL ADVANCEMENT FOUNDATION INTERNATIONAL

The Foundation cultivates markets, policies and communities that support thriving, socially just, and environmentally sound family farms. Their grant program assists farmers and rural communities in developing new sources of agricultural income through the provision of cost-share grants. The program awards grants of up to $8,000 to individual farmers, or $10,000 to collaborative farmer projects in NORTH CAROLINA. Priority will be given to projects that demonstrate a way to replace lost tobacco income. Eligible counties change each year, so be sure to check the website. Application deadline of December 15th. See website for details.
See: www.rafiusa.org/grants/

SAGINAW BAY WATERSHED INITIATIVE NETWORK

The Network seeks to advance the search for sustainable solutions to current watershed and community challenges within the Saginaw Bay MICHIGAN watershed which includes 22 counties. Their focus includes Agriculture, Pollution Prevention and Land Use. No deadlines. See: www.saginawbaywin.org/grants/

SAND COUNTY FOUNDATION

The Foundation's Leopold Conservation Award Program recognizes agricultural landowners actively committed to a land ethic. The best example of voluntary conservation by a private landowner is awarded $10,000 each year through the program, which is currently available in CALIFORNIA, COLORADO, KENTUCKY, NEBRASKA, SOUTH DAKOTA, TEXAS, UTAH, WISCONSIN and WYOMING. Award criteria includes responsible management, sustainable revenue, leadership, overall land health, innovation and outreach. Applications varies by state. See: www.leopoldconservationaward.org

SCOTTS MIRACLE GRO CO.

The company's GRO1000 Grassroots Grants are intended to foster community spirit and public service. Grants range in amount from $500 to $1,500 and are offered to non-profit organizations, school districts, universities and government entities to help bring edible gardens, flower gardens and public green spaces to neighborhoods across the UNITED STATES. February deadline. See website for application details.
See: www.grogood.com/GiveBackToGro/Gro1000/Grassroots

ALICE WILSON SCHWEITZER & WM. J. SCHWEITZER AGRICULTURE EDUCATION FOUNDATION

Scholarships to ILLINOIS students for agriculture studies. Deadline of June 30th. Write: Jane Hartley Pratt 57 Public Square PO Box 200 Monmouth, IL 61462

SEED TO FOOD

The organization's Hoop House Grant Program provided matching grants for the construction of one or more hoop houses in Kenosha, Racine or Walworth Counties of WISCONSIN. Organization also maintains a list of other funding sources.
See: www.seedtofood.com/financial

SEEDS OF CHANGE®

The organization's grant program is designed to give communities the ingredients to grow a healthier, more sustainable relationship with food by supporting sustainable community-based gardening and farming programs within the UNITED STATES. Grants of $20,000 and $10,000 are awarded each year to fund programs the organization sees as the best examples of enhancing the environmental, economic, and social well-being of gardens, farms, farmers and communities. Non-profit organizations with a focus on food and/or farming, in addition to local community organizations may apply. Deadline of March 31st. See website for application details.
See: www.seedsofchangegrant.com/

CALCOT – SEITZ FOUNDATION

The Foundation offers scholarships each year to students pursuing a career in agriculture. Scholarships are ordinarily awarded in amounts between $1,000 and $3,000. Applicants must be agriculture students from CALIFORNIA, NEW MEXICO, TEXAS or ARIZONA cotton-growing areas. The Foundation also provides grants for scientific and economic research activities, such as on-campus seed research labs and computer learning centers in agricultural business and economics departments. See website for application details.
See: www.calcot.com

SHADEFUND

Established by The Conservation Fund with a lead grant from the U.S. Endowment for Forestry and Communities, the ShadeFund enables others to invest in green entrepreneurs across the UNITED STATES to grow their businesses and create jobs. Tax deductible contributions to ShadeFund are pooled and lent to qualified small green businesses nationwide. As entrepreneurs repay the loans, those same dollars are recycled to help other entrepreneurs grow their businesses. Businesses (such as farmers, woodworkers, restaurants, agri-tourism, etc.) that use natural resources sustainably may apply for loans ranging from $5,000 to $50,000 toward equipment or working capital. See: www.shadefund.org

SIMPLY ORGANIC® 1% FUND

Frontier's all-organic brand, Simply Organic® funds many worthy organizations and events that support organics and encourage and support the growth of organic and sustainable agriculture. They fund research and education initiatives that champion organic agriculture and meet the goals of the organization best. No deadlines.
See: www.simplyorganic.com/simplyorganic/ourvalues/applying.php

SLOW FOOD UPSTATE GRANTS

Slow Food Upstate's $300 grants are awarded to help toward project costs that advance food and nutrition education and are intended to further the professional development of their region's educators, students enrolled in schools or Colleges and Universities public or private, farmers and food producers, chefs and restaurant owners, fishers, agricultural historians, ranchers, nurserymen and conservation activist in the Upstate region of SOUTH CAROLINA and which celebrate create public awareness of the area's diverse biological, cultural and culinary heritage. June 1st deadline. See: www.slowfoodupstate.com/grants.htm

J.A. & FLOSSIE MAE SMITH SCHOLARSHIP FUND
The Fund awards scholarships up to $2,500, which may be renewable, to students studying agriculture at a CALIFORNIA college or university. There is no deadline. See website for application details.
See: www.sdfoundation.org/SanDiegoCenterforCharitableGiving.aspx

SOLIDAGO
The foundation makes grants to address unjust systems such as disparities in wealth, resources, power and opportunity, with Environmental Justice being an area of particular interest. Progressive organizations may apply.
See: www.solidago.org

SOUTHERN MINNESOTA INITIATIVE FOUNDATION
The Foundation's Incentive Grants program supports new asset-based collaborative approaches in MINNESOTA that demonstrate measurable results related to economic development. Grants amount up to $20,000. Submission deadlines are in February and August. Application information can be found online.
See: www.smifoundation.org/

SOUTHERN MARYLAND AGRICULTURAL DEVELOPMENT COMMISSION
The Commission is offering grants to farms in specific MARYLAND counties. Viability Grants are intended to foster ways to increase the income and sustainability of area farms, among other reasons. Grants ranget from $5,000 to $40,000 with 1:1 matching funds. The Growing Grapes for Wine program was established to encourage and support the development of a competitive wine industry in Southern Maryland. Eligible applicants own or co-own at least 5 acres of land currently being used for agriculture. See website for application details.
See: www.SMADC.com

SOUTHERN OHIO AGRICULTURAL & COMMUNITY DEVELOPMENT FOUNDATION

The Foundation provides educational assistance, as well as agricultural and economic development grants in southern OHIO. Their Competitive Grant Program is intended for full-time enrolled sophomores, juniors or seniors with a current Farm Service Number on record with the Farm Service Agency at the time of application OR tobacco quota owners, quota owners/growers, or grower/tenants of Farm Service Agency record in any single crop year from 1997 to 2004, and their immediate family dependents, that are enrolled at an accredited institution and are seeking a Bachelor's degree. Application deadline of January 31st. See website for application details.
See: www.soacdf.net

SOUTHERN UNITED STATES TRADE ASSOCIATION

The Association's Market Access Program Brand was designed for small businesses in the UNITED STATES that desire financial support to launch a new branded export effort. The Association will reimburse up to 50% of certain international marketing and promotion expenses. Applications are accepted on a rolling basis with more information found online.
See: www.susta.org/services/map.html

SOUTHWEST GEORGIA FARM CREDIT

The organization's "Fresh from the Farm" grant program awards local farmers markets in GEORGIA $500 each to help ensure continued distribution of locally-grown products as well as stimulation of the local economy. See website for application information and current deadlines.
See: www.swgafarmcredit.com/news/conferences-and-grants/fresh-from-the-farm.aspx

SOW IT FORWARD
Kitchen Gardeners International is accepting applications for the Sow It Forward grant program. The program is for non-profit organizations nationwide working to start or expand food garden projects that benefit to the community. The grant packages (averaging $500) are a mix of cash and access to products. January deadline. See website for application details.
See: www.kgi.org/grants

Specialty Food Foundation™
The Specialty Food Foundation™ develops and supports tangible and lasting solutions to hunger and food recovery, amplifying the innovation and passion of the specialty food industry.   The vision is a community of social entrepreneurs breaking the hunger cycle and enriching life. Letters of inquiry are submitted by email in early spring; those selected receive invites to apply.   Grants are in the form of seed grants, operating, innovation, project and capacity building ranging in size from $5,000 to $30,000.
See: www.specialtyfoodfoundation.org

SURDNA FOUNDATION
The Surdna Foundation partners with local and national non-profit organizations within the UNITED STATES to foster just and sustainable communities by making grants in the areas of sustainable environments (including food security), strong local economies, thriving cultures and foundation initiatives. No deadlines. See website for application details. See: www.surdna.org/grants/grants-overview.html

SUSTAINABLE AGRICULTURE RESEARCH & EDUCATION (SARE)

SARE's mission is to advance — to the whole of AMERICAN agriculture — innovations that improve profitability, stewardship and quality of life by investing in groundbreaking research and education. U.S. researchers, agricultural educators, students, farmers and ranchers can apply. Grant projects might explore topics like On-Farm renewable energy, Pest and weed management, Pastured livestock & rotational grazing, No-till and conservation tillage,Nutrient management, Agroforestry, Marketing, Sustainable communities, Systems research,Crop and livestock diversity, and more! Applicants apply in their own geographic region. See: www.sare.org;

Northeast SARE - www.nesare.org/Grants/Get-a-Grant;
Northcentral SARE -
 www.northcentralsare.org/Grants/Our-Grant-Programs;
Western SARE - www.westernsare.org/Grants/Types-of-Grants;
Eastern SARE - www.southernsare.org/Grants/Grant-Deadlines

SYNGENTA FOUNDATION

The Foundation's Grow More Vegetables Seed Grants provide grants and in-kind donations to non-profits, schools and government agencies in the UNITED STATES for the establishment of gardens that facilitate education of local communities. Projects should promote principles of growing food, promoting biodiversity, health, and reducing waste, poverty and environmental degradation. Recipients receive donations of vegetable seed and a monetary award. Deadline of September 15th. Applications online. See: www.syngenta-us.com/home.aspx

TENNESSEE FARM BUREAU
The Bureau helps teachers present agriculture curriculum to students in TENNESSEE by providing grants of up to $500 for Outdoor Classroom Gardens. The mini-grants are designed to show that agriculture is an integral part of our everyday environment. Schools, 4-H Clubs and chapters of the FFA may apply, but matching funds are necessary. No deadlines to apply. See website for application details.
See: www.tnfarmbureau.org/content/grants-tours

TEXAS DEPARTMENT OF AGRICULTURE
The Department's Young Farmer Grant program aims to grow and support Texas agriculture by helping to meet financial needs and grow operations that impact the community. Matching grants of $5,000 to $10,000 are offered twice a year to young TEXAS producers (18-45 years old) who are starting or expanding an agricultural business. Applications accepted in the Spring and Fall of each year. See website for application details.
See: www.texasagriculture.gov/GrantsServices.aspx

TEXAS WATER DEVELOPMENT BOARD
The Board's mission is to provide leadership, information, education, and support for planning, financial assistance, and outreach for the conservation and responsible development of water for TEXAS. There are three categories: Agricultural Water Conservation Monitoring with metering, Agricultural Water Conservation Monitoring by other measurement, and Agricultural Irrigation System Improvements. Amounts of up to $2,100,000 are available to political subdivisions, state agencies, and state institutions of higher learning with a deadline of September 10th. See: www.twdb.texas.gov/about/contract_admin/rfq/RFA_Ag Grants.asp

THE BURT'S BEES GREATER GOOD FOUNDATION
The Foundation supports programs for sustainable and urban agriculture and community gardening to achieve improved human health through nutrition and food security, improved environmental sustainability and supporting the community and local economy. (See website for more details.) Most grant awards are made to North Carolina organizations.
See: burtsbees.com

THE TORO FOUNDATION
The Toro Foundation makes grants that benefit agriculture and the environment, among other causes, primarily in areas where the company has operations such as CALIFORNIA, MISSISSIPPI, MINNESOTA, NEBRASKA, TEXAS and WISCONSIN. The company accepts requests from non-profit organizations for equipment and irrigation donations January through March each year. See website for program details.
See: www.thetorocompany.com

UNFI FOUNDATION
The Foundation fund innovative new programs which support the development of healthy, organic foods and food practices. Past awards have helped to increase organic food production, provide research and science to develop organic farming practices, protect the biodiversity of our seed supply and the stewardship of genetic resources of organic seed, support transparent labeling, teach organic farming practices that promote conservation of resources, foster the next generation of organic farmers, provide nutrition education, and host forums and conferences. Non-profit organizations in the UNITED STATES maysubmi a letter of intent in September, January or April.
See: www.unfifoundation.org

THE UNITED STATES CONFERENCE OF MAYORS

The Conference's Gardens and Green Spaces Grant Program is intended to support garden and green space development in American cities. The program also intends to make community garden strategies stronger and with more continuing to pop up around the country in order to streamline the operation and make it as fruitful as possible. Projects to be funded should add a new or substantial addition to an existing public garden or green space within the city. Projects should also engage area residents, be transformative in scope, serve as a focal point/visible project for the city, impact the lives of the city's citizens and serve as an essential portion of the city's sustainability plan. Local government officials are eligible with 5 awards totaling up to $40,000 available. Check the website in the summer for fall submission.
See: www.usmayors.org/gro1000/

UNIVERSITY OF ARKANSAS - STRAWBERRY

The University's National Strawberry Sustainability Initiative is intended to move sustainable production forward through innovation, application of new technology, demonstration, outreach/extension, and education, ultimately resulting in increased sustainable production and supply of strawberries to American consumers. Land-grant colleges and universities or state funded public universities and colleges may apply. Grants range in amount from $50,000 to $200,000. see website for application details.
See: www.strawberry.uark.edu

UNIVERSITY OF MASSACHUSETTS

The University's Sustainable Food and Farming Program lists grants and scholarships through their website for use by students and/or other interested parties.
See: www.sustfoodfarm.org/2014/10/27/grants/

URANN FOUNDATION
The foundation awards scholarships to students studying agriculture who come from cranberry producing families in MASSACHUSETTS. The deadline is April 15th.
Write: PO Box 1802 Providence, RI 02901

U.S. COMPOSTING COUNCIL
The Council founded the Young Investigator Scholarship to support a young professional's research in the fields of compost use and application for soil conservation effort. Undergraduate through PhD level students whose research and interests focus on composting may apply through December 12th. Recipient will be awarded funds to support their research and education. See website for application details.
See: www.compostingcouncil.org/scholarships/

U.S. POULTRY & EGG HAROLD E. FORD FOUNDATION
The Poultry Science Education Fund supports student recruitment at colleges and universities with poultry science courses that do not have a full department with a poultry science degree. A committee of poultry science school professionals will evaluate funding requests and make recommendations to the Board of Directors of the U.S. Poultry Foundation. Any institution of higher education in the United States that offers an identifiable poultry science program is eligible to apply before August 1st for a recruitment grant of up to $7,000. See website for application details.
See: www.poultryfoundation.org

UTOPIA FOUNDATION

The Foundation's mission is to help create a world where communities thrive and every child goes to bed feeling nourished, loved, happy and hopeful about tomorrow. Utopia Gifts is a matching grant and fiduciary program through the Foundation. The Foundation identifies and partners with non-profit programs that align with their mission and have a high probability of success. Grant opportunities change regularly, so check their website for current opportunities. See website for application details.
See: www.utopiafound.org

LAWSON VALENTINE FOUNDATION

The foundation makes awards for the environment, economic justice, food systems, and sustainable agriculture. Gives primarily in CONNECTICUT, NEW JERSEY, NEW YORK and CALIFORNIA. Awards range from $500 to $50,000. no deadlines.
Write: 1000 Farmington Avenue, Suite 105A West Hartford, Connecticut 06107.

VANCITY

The credit union provides Small Growers Loans to producers of viable and sustainable local food systems in CANADA which contribute to a stronger economy. The loans are designed to help farm businesses get off the ground. Loans of up to $75,000 are available at competitive rates. Loans are intended for individual or cooperative owners farming under 50 acres who are working the land or growing food in other ways. See website for application details.
See: www.vancity.com/BusinessBanking/

JULIA VANDER MAY BAKELAAR CHARITABLE TRUST

The Trust makes grants nationwide for the purposes of supporting education programs for handicapped children, health, human and social service programs run by churches, and community based food programs. Interested applicants should submit a proposal detailing the use of funds and the amount of funding requested. Applicants must be a non-profit organization. Grants of up to $20,000 are available. No application deadline. The trust does not have a website at this time.
Write: William Hanse 2035 E. Hamburg Turnpike Wayne, NJ 07470-6251

VELA FOUNDATION

The Foundation is dedicated to promoting improved nutrition and wellness in eastern MASSACHUSETTS, with an emphasis on underserved communities. They support non-profit organizations whose missions include nutrition literacy and education, improved fitness and increasing access to healthy foods. Deadlines in March and September. See website for application details.
See: www.velafoundation.org

VERMONT AGENCY OF AGRICULTURE, FOOD & MARKETS

The Agency's Best Management Practice Program is designed to provide state financial assistance to farmers in VERMONT. Funding is intended for the voluntary construction of on-farm improvements designed to abate non-point source agricultural waste discharges into the waters of the state. Funding can be combined with federal cost share to provide a maximum of 85% of an approved project. Applications are accepted year-round. Vermont has grants available for Farm to School as well as Local Farm Market Development. Click on the Grants tab.
See: www.agriculture.vermont.gov

VERMONT DEPARTMENT OF HEALTH – GREEN THUMBS AT WORK

The Department is working with the Vermont Community Garden Network to provide "Green Thumbs at Work" grants for small businesses with fewer than 50 employees in VERMONT to establish workplace food gardens. Total grant award in 2015 was $1,750 with $500 being allocated for materials, $250 in the form of a gift certificate to Gardener's Supply and $1,000 of garden planning support and technical assistance from a horticulturalist and the Vermont Community Garden Network. Gardens can be in-ground or raised beds. The employees must be the primary users of the garden and beneficiaries of the food. Eight grants awarded per year with an application deadline of January 30th.
See: www.vcgn.org/green-thumbs-at-work

VERMONT FARM & FOREST VIABILITY PROGRAM

The Program assists VERMONT dairy farm members of the St. Albans Co-op to make a wide variety of infrastructure investments that will increase milk production and farm viability with grants of up to $40,000. Applications due by December 18th.
See: www.vhcb.org/Farm-Forest-Viability/dairy-grants/

VERMONT LEGISLATURE

The Legislature's Vermont Barn Grant Program provides competitive 50/50 matching grants of up to $15,000 for the repair of historic agricultural buildings. Qualified parties must have a 50-year-old structure (or more) with eligibility for the National Register of Historic Places. Application deadline of November 5th.
See:
www.accd.vermont.gov/strong_communities/preservation/grants/barn

WALLACE GENETIC FOUNDATION

The Wallace Genetic Foundation promotes sustainable agriculture, farmland preservation, conservation of natural resources, biodiversity protection, reduction of environmental toxins, and global climate issues. The grants offered usually range from $25,000 to $50,000. Applications are due by November 1st. See website for application details.
See: www.wallacegenetic.org

WASHINGTON APPLE EDUCATION FOUNDATION

The Washington Apple Education Foundation provides educational opportunities, encourages academic excellence and promotes awareness of the values of Washington's Tree Fruit Industry. The Foundation offers scholarships around $2,500 to students in WASHINGTON. March 1st deadline. See website for application details.
See: www.waef.org/scholarships/

WESTERN GROWERS FOUNDATION

The Foundation's Arizona School Garden Program is intended to support the creation of sustainable fruit and vegetable gardens at ARIZONA and CALIFORNIA K-12 schools. Grants are provided for programs that will use garden-enhanced education to illuminate for students where their food comes from as well as the importance of good nutrition. Grants amount $1,500 each. Deadline of March 31st. See website for application details.
See: www.wga.com/services/foundation

WESTERN NEW YORK REGIONAL ECONOMIC DEVELOPMENT COUNCIL

The Council's Agriculture Development Fund is designed for farmers in Western NEW YORK to apply for assistance with processing equipment purchases and constructing or renovating agricultural structures. Grants do not generally exceed $50,000 and are available to agricultural producers with commercial farms. No deadlines posted. See website for application details.
See: www.regionalcouncils.ny.gov/western-new-york/103014/edenvalley

WESTERN NORTH CAROLINA AG-OPTIONS

The organization strives to protect mountain farmland by assisting the longevity of farm enterprises. AgOptions funds farmers in NORTH CAROLINA who are diversifying or expanding their operations grants between $3,000 and $6,000 in order to offset the risk of trying a new venture. Deadline of November 21st. See website for application details.
See: www.wncagoptions.org

WHOLE FOODS MARKET

The company provides many grants and loans for different entities within the UNITED STATES. Their Whole Kids Foundation makes grants to schools and teachers to provide gardening and salad bar opportunities for all. Their Community Giving program donates funding to non-profit and educational organizations on their semi-annual "5% Days." The company's Local Producer Loan Program provides low-interest loans to small, local producers that bring more local products to market. Grant and loan amounts vary by program. See website for application details.
See: www.wholefoodsmarket.com/mission-values/caring-communities

PEARY WILEMAN NATIONAL COTTON GINNERS SCHOLARSHIP

Scholarships are awarded to students with a minimum of sophomore level whose studies are related to the cotton ginning industry. Deadline of February 1st. See website for application details.

See: www.cotton.org/ncga/scholarship/index.cfm

THE WILBUR & BIRDIE WILLIAMS TRUST

The trust awards scholarships to agricultural undergraduate students from Johnson County, WYOMING. Deadline of April 1st.

Write: PO Box 400, Buffalo, WY 82834

WILLISTON STAR FUND

The Fund's Community Enhancement Grant is intended to take mini steps to make Williston, NORTH DAKOTA a better place by helping new and existing businesses to succeed, make their properties more attractive to their customers, and to make the community more attractive to potential new businesses, employees, residents and visitors. The STAR Fund will match the investment of any non-profit group in commercial and industrial zoned property projects on a 1:2 basis with a maximum of $10,000 per project. Applicant's minimum out of pocket project expense shall total $20,000, with a mini-match cap of $200,000 per calendar year available. Deadline of December 15th. See website for application details.

See: www.willistonwire.com/Programs/Williston-STAR-Fund

WISCONSIN FARM BUREAU FEDERATION

The Federation's mission is to provide agricultural resources for teachers, students and volunteers in WISCONSIN. The organization's Teacher Mini-Grants are provided in amounts of up to $100 each to preschool through high school teachers, in a public or private school system, to fund projects that promote agricultural literacy in the classroom. Projects should focus on integrating agriculture into a variety of curriculum
areas. Deadline of October 15th. Applications can be found online.
See: www.wisagclassroom.org/programs-activities/grants/teacher-mini-grants/

WISCONSIN STATE RABBIT BREEDERS ASSOCIATION

The Association's grant program's main objective is to promote and perpetuate the rabbit hobby or industry in WISCONSIN. The Entrepreneurial Grant is designed to provide a youth member (14 to 20 years of age) of the WSRBA with funding to develop and work through a project that will benefit the WSRBA, it's members and/or the rabbit industry in WI. Applicants will be judged on the impact the proposed project has on others. Grants range in amount from $100 to $500. deadline of July 1st. See website for application details.
See:
www.wsrba.org/images/WSRBAentrepreneurgrantNew2009.pdf

WOMEN'S NATIONAL FARM AND GARDEN ASSOCIATION, INC.

Women's National Farm and Garden Association offers access to scholarships, internships, fellowships, sponsorships, and grants to those interested in horticulture.
See: www.wnfga.org

WORKING LANDS ENTERPRISE INITIATIVE
The Initiative is intended to manage and invest funding into the agricultural and forestry-based businesses in VERMONT. There are three categories of investments: Working Lands Enterprise, Service Provider Grants and Capital and Infrastructure. Deadlines, grantees and amounts vary by category. See website for application details.
See: www.workinglands.vermont.gov

WORLD FOOD PRIZE FOUNDATION
The foundation makes research awards and prizes to individuals who have advance human development by improving the quality, quantity, or availability of food in the world. Academic and research institutions, private or public organizations, corporate entities or units of government may submit nominations. The award of $250,000 is presented in October, with an application deadline of May 1st. See website for details on the application and nomination process.
See: www.worldfoodprize.org

WWOOF-USA
The organization's Small Farm Grant Program awards grants to WWOOF-USA hosts for special projects intended to further their mission, enhance the educational experience of visiting WWOOFers on farms, and promote small-scale organic agriculture and land stewardship.
See: www.wwoofusa.org

WYOMING FARMERS MARKETS

The organization's Specialty Crop Program High Tunnel Grants are awarded to non-profit organizations and educational institutions to promote Specialty Crop season extension through high tunnel projects. Agricultural organizations within WYOMING are eligible to apply for matching grants of between $500 and $3,500. July 1st deadline.

See: www.wyagric.state.wy.us

OTHER RESOURCES:

Here are some special **Technical Assistance Providers**:

AGRICULTURAL MARKETING RESOURCE CENTER (AGMRC) is a national center providing information on value-added commodities and business development information. Additionally, AgMRC provides individual contacts within each state on value-added programs. Some of these programs may contain grant opportunities specific to that state.
See: www.agmrc.org

THE CENTER FOR RURAL AFFAIRS promotes healthy, local foods and food systems through policy, research, education, and direct work with farmers and others who produce and distribute food. Service initiatives include helping new farmers access land and financing, including loans, building local food systems through farmers markets and community networks, and educating on sustainable practices. Sign up for free newsletter on website.
See: www.cfra.org/resources/beginning_farmer

MICHIGAN FOOD & FARMING SYSTEMS (MIFFS) is a statewide, non-profit organization whose purpose is to improve Michigan's triple bottom line: economy, environment and the social well-being of communities by promoting family farms, local food and sustainable agriculture. The mission is to connect beginning and historically underserved farmers to resource opportunities for developing profitable and environmentally sustainable livelihoods.
See: www.miffs.org

PATTY CANTRELL of REGIONAL FOOD SOLUTIONS, LLC
Communications, strategic planning, project development
Focus: Local food as community and economic development
RFS can help projects nationwide to engage & motivate community stakeholders
Call 231-794-1792 or Email: patty@regionalfoodsolutions.com
See: regionalfoodsolutions.com

GOVERNMENT AND COMMUNITY GRANTS

Go to your state or province's or municipality's webpage and look for food or farming grants - possibly under the Department of Agriculture or Department of Health or Economic Development. The application process differs state to state. U.S. residents may wish to check www.usda.gov and www.Start2Farm.gov as well as your own State's USDA office, Department of Agriculture, Land Grant University agriculture professionals, local cooperative extension office, granges, farm bureaus, and/or the crop or producer associations in your state for opportunities.

UNITED STATES DEPT OF AGRICULTURE (USDA)

- The Department's **Value-Added Producer Grants** are designed to help agricultural producers in the UNITED STATES enter into value-added activities related to the processing and/or marketing of bio-based value-added products. Their goal is to generate new products, create and expand marketing opportunities and increase producer income. Priority is given to new farmers or ranchers, socially-disadvantaged farmers or ranchers, small or medium-sized farms or ranches structured as a family farm and farmer or rancher coops. Grants vary in amount depending on the project. (See: http://www.rd.usda.gov/programs-services/value-added-producer-grants)

- The Healthy, Hunger-Free Kids Act of 2010 (HHFKA) amended Section 18 of the Richard B. Russell National School Lunch Act (NSLA) to establish a Farm to School Program in order to assist eligible entities, through grants and technical assistance, in implementing farm to school programs that improve access to local foods in eligible schools. To fulfill the farm to the HHFKA school mandate, the United States Department of Agriculture (USDA) offers grants and technical assistance through the **Farm to School Program**. This request for applications (RFA) provides additional details regarding the grants component. The USDA Food and Nutrition Service (FNS) is charged with implementing the Farm to School Program. (See: http://www.fns.usda.gov/farmtoschool/farm-school)

- The Department's **Agricultural Management Assistance Organic Certification Cost Share Program** is available to producers of crops and livestock in CONNECTICUT, DELAWARE, HAWAII, MAINE, MARYLAND, MASSACHUSETTS, NEVADA, NEW HAPSHIRE, NEW JERSEY, NEW YORK, PENNSYLVANIA, RHODE ISLAND, UTAH, VERMONT, WEST VIRGINIA and WYOMING. Operations must possess current USDA organic certification to be eligible to receive reimbursements. Grants of up to $2,250 are available for applications received before December 31st. See website for application details. Through the Department's Environmental Quality Incentives Program, Seasonal High Tunnel Systems for Crops through the Natural Resources Conservation Service may be available for agricultural producers in the UNITED STATES to extend the growing season in an environmentally safe manner. Applications are accepted on a continuous basis, though individual states may establish deadlines. Individuals, legal entities, Indian Tribes, or joint operations, as well as organic producers with eligible land may apply. See website for application details. See: www.rurdev.usda.gov/bcp_vapg.html and www.ams.usda.gov and www.nrcs.usda.gov/wps/portal/nrcs/detailfull/national/programs/?cid=stelprdb1046250.

- The Office's **Outreach and Assistance for Socially Disadvantaged Farmers and Ranchers and Veteran Farmers and Ranchers Program** is designed to assist the socially disadvantaged, veteran farmers and ranchers in owning and operating farms and ranches in the UNITED STATES while increasing their participation in agricultural programs and services provided by the USDA. Community-based organizations, higher education institutions, and tribal entities may apply. See: http://www.outreach.usda.gov/grants/index.htm.

- **Other USDA funding initiatives include the Specialty Crop Block Grant Program (**Specialty crops are defined as fruits and vegetables, tree nuts, dried fruits, and nursery crops - including floriculture), the **Farmers Market Promotion Program** helps to promote farmers markets including the ability to process EBT cards, local producers using community kitchen facilities, where food can be processed, stored and transported, and the **Local Food Promotion Program that** supports the development and expansion of local and regional food business enterprises to increase domestic consumption of, and access to, locally and regionally produced agricultural products, and to develop new market opportunities for farm and ranch operations serving local markets with both planning and implementation funding.
(See: ams.usda.gov/AMSv1.0/AMSgrants)

NATURAL RESOURCES CONSERVATION SERVICE
The NRCS offers voluntary programs to eligible landowners and agricultural producers to provide financial and technical assistance to help manage natural resources in a sustainable manner. The agency will approve contracts to provide financial assistance to help plan and implement conservation practices that address natural resource concerns or

opportunities to help save energy, improve soil, water, plant, air, animal and related resources on agricultural lands and non-industrial private forest land. At present, there are three categories of financial programs.
See:
www.nrcs.usda.gov/wps/portal/nrcs/main/national/prog rams/financial/

ADMINISTRATION FOR CHILDREN AND FAMILIES
The administration's Refugee Agricultural Grant Program intends to fund programs that propose strategies which incorporate agriculture and food systems to improve the lives of refugee families. The strategies should result in sustainable and/or supplemental income, improved access to healthy foods and better nutrition, and enhanced integration into communities by refugee families. Deadline is in July. See website for application details.
See: www.acf.hhs.gov/grants/open/foa/view/HHS-2013-ACF-ORR-ZR-0571

Some local, city and county governments have made allocations to support community gardens or farm markets. A rural municipality might look into federal USDA Community Facility grants for renovations or construction. Also check the National Institute of Food and Agriculture www.csrees.usda.gov/fo/recentReleasedGrants.cfm for grant opportunities.

Entrepreneurial farmers may wish to check their state's Heritage or Historical Preservation resources for help toward maintaining old structures on the farm. Also look for Conservation, Green Energy and Environmental funders. Most grant makers only give to 501c3 nonprofit organizations; entrepreneurial farmers may be written into a nonprofit's applications as a contractual provider to perform certain tasks in a project.

Some community foundations have funded specific one-time costs for community or school gardens or markets. You may also contact your area's community foundation and see if your project is eligible. A community foundation may pay for a new computer or renovation but may not pay for operational costs.

Some area garden and horticulture clubs also make grants available.

BE WRITTEN INTO OTHER'S GRANTS

Ask to be written in as a contractual provider or demonstration site in grants being submitted by land grant universities, states, statewide or larger organizations.

As a model check and see how the group eOrganic at www.eXtension.org/organic_production – note eXtension (pronounced e-extension) framed their resources and proposal needs.

See: www.eorganic.info/proposal

CLOSED GRANTS

Some Foundations may only give to preselected organizations or publicize that no applications will be accepted. In this case, if they are in your service area, you may wish to keep an eye on their activities and note whether the trustees, areas of interest and application process changes over time. And in some cases it may be appropriate to add the trustees or foundation to your organization's newsletter mailing list. Some foundations' assets change over time. Some foundations change as the next generation assumes leadership. You may want to check their website or 990 each year to see if they have resumed giving to applicants.

FUNDRAISING

Many foundations like to see that your nonprofit has already raised some funds toward your project. If a grant maker asks for a budget and expects a local match – that is the money you raised from other sources. Example: If you are proposing a $10,000 project, for example, and the funder requires a 10% local match, you will need to show that you have already raised $1,000 through fundraising for this the project and are requesting a grant of $9,000.

Nonprofits raise funds in multiple ways - events, annual gifts, memorials, online giving, etc. Do you ask donors for the name and address of the person(s) to be notified if a donor makes a gift in honor or in memory of someone? Do you send out a year end annual appeal letter by mail or email to past supporters (past donors, volunteers, current and past staff, current and past board members, vendors, past and current interns, etc.)

Busy people and those that act on impulse enjoy e-giving – it is quick and easy. Do you have a Paypal™ Donate Now button on your webpage? Or are you able to receive donations via smart phones and receive PCI compliant donations (meeting Payment Card Industry Data Security Standards to ensure security)? People can make gifts easily using Network for Good (www.networkforgood.com) among others. The donation minus a transaction fee is deposited directly into your nonprofit's bank account. Be sure to read all the instructions and agreement language. You also may wish to look into accepting donations via QR codes or Electronic Funds Transfer (EFT). You can even set up monthly gifts instead of onetime gifts.

Other sources of funding for nonprofits or farmers raising money for food or farming projects may include social media fundraising such using
Razoo (www.razoo.com/p/for_nonprofits) or www.givefor ward.com,
www.fundrazr.com, www.fundraisingforacause.com, www. crowdrise.com,
www.indiegogo.com, www.zip.kiva.org, www.justgive.org, etc. Be sure to check and compare transaction fees.

You can also promote a fundraising event using a site like EventBrite. (Note there is even a way for people who cannot attend the event to make a donation without buying a ticket. (See: www.eventbrite.com/l/npo/.) Consider cause marketing with area businesses (local businesses or corporations agree to give some $ for each item sold to your cause; the business gets good publicity, your group gets some money.)

A pay it forward program allows people to pay their bill and then pay the fee for the next customer. A feed and seed store may agree to Pay it Forward for a farmer.

Register your nonprofit at org.amazon.com (See: www.smile.amazon.com/about) to secure donations from Amazon shoppers from the AmazonSmile™ Foundation. Then spread the word among your supporters (electronically) that if they shop Amazon to log in using smile.amazon.com and then select your charity Amazon Smile Foundation will make a contribution to your organization.

Nonprofits can also update their profile on GuideStar.org. Potential donors may search GuideStar looking for organization's whose causes fit their values. Donors may make a gift through GuideStar (See: www.guidestar.org/rxg/help/faqs/on-line-donations/index.aspx#faq1812.) Create an account and claim your nonprofit, then click on update Nonprofit Report to set up your organization's profile. Fill out the GuideStar Exchange Form (GX) to provide additional information about your organization including uploading documents.

STAY IN TOUCH

To be added to a mailing list about future nonprofit management or fundraising tools, please share your information by emailing info@grant-write.com or writing Pamela Burke, P.O. Box 291, Remus, Michigan 49340.

Also feel free to share a summary of your successful funding strategies.

ABOUT THE AUTHOR

The author, Pamela Burke, has worked with, and for, nonprofit and charitable organizations her entire life. She began searching for funding and writing grants in 1978 – first as a volunteer, later as an employee, and for the last two decades as a self-employed grant writer and fund development consultant. As a technical assistance provider her mission is to improve the quality of life in communities by building the organizational capacity of nonprofits – especially those serving rural areas. When not working, you can find her planning her next trip, working in the garden, dabbling in the arts, kayaking and volunteering.

Made in the USA
Lexington, KY
12 November 2015